Earth,

The Improbable Utopia

Written by R. J. Fidalgo

While every precaution has been taken in the preparation of this book, the publisher assumes no responsibility for errors or omissions, or for damages resulting from the use of the information contained herein.

EARTH, THE IMPROBABLE UTOPIA

First edition. November 1, 2024.

Copyright © 2024 R. J. Fidalgo.

Written by R. J. Fidalgo.

Table of Content

Preface

After finishing my first book, "*The Life and Spiritual Journey of No One,*" I was often met with curious and natural questions: 'Are you going to write another? Do you have a new project in the works?' My immediate thought was always, 'No, I'm not that kind of author.' I don't fabricate stories, nor do I write books to get rich—if that were my goal, I'd surely be in the wrong line of business.

While I enjoy exploring matters of the heart and consciousness, I don't have a particular love for writing. My journey as a writer has been driven by a series of circumstances that led me to it, rather than by a deep-seated passion for the craft itself. I thought I was finished after the first book, but once again, I felt compelled to write about something important, which turned out to be a natural sequel to the first. On the other hand, engaging in this work granted me a deeper connection, as Light filled me in the most gentle and fulfilling way, serving as a sort of validation.

I will strive to make this book stand on its own, though reading the first one will undoubtedly provide a deeper understanding. If nothing else, this book will offer an intriguing read. But who knows? Perhaps it will become something more.

Introduction

The idea of creating Heaven on Earth is one that many of you have likely encountered, yet for most, it probably feels more like a cosmic joke than a genuine possibility. The truth is, the world is what we make it—and unfortunately, we haven't made it a very nice place. We seem trapped in a loop where we kill and feed off each other, and the odds of this ending well appear slim.

Our collective choices have brought us to this point, making the prospect of a utopian future seem like nothing more than a distant mirage. While such a future might seem highly improbable, I assure you that it is possible. Through the course of this book, I will show you how.

I will draw on various subjects and perspectives from different cultures, religions, traditions, and governments to highlight both the good and the bad. By addressing a wide range of topics, I'll present examples worth following and confront many of the issues that plague our societies. However, you'll come to realize, as I have, that there will never be a perfect solution to the problems of imperfect societies. A new approach is necessary.

In these pages, I will explore how things are, how they could be, and how we might get there. My goal is to make the impossible feasible through a series of steps. Taking these steps will not be easy, especially because we must take them together. But that's to be expected when striving for such radical change.

Ultimately, this endeavor will depend greatly on opportunity—an opportunity that may never come. But if it does, may we seize it to create something truly great and beautiful for all mankind.

Chapter One
Our Planetary Context

Star systems are the cradles of life, and within them exist planets with the potential to nurture life. Not all planets within a system possess this potential, but those that do have the opportunity to progress through the cycles of evolution. There are, in essence, seven cycles of evolution, or planes of existence, and they are: First, the Cycle of Awakening; Second, the Cycle of Growth; Third, the Cycle of Self-Awareness; Fourth, the Cycle of Love and Understanding; Fifth, the Cycle of Wisdom; Sixth, the Cycle of Unity; and Seventh, the Cycle of Ascension.

At a certain point, a trigger touches a planetary sphere with such potential, and things begin to move. In the Cycle of Awakening, the primordial elements commence their intricate dance, which, over a very long period of time, will create the first expression of life: bacteria. This event marks the beginning of the Cycle of Growth, where different expressions of life evolve in a harmonious and balanced fashion. Life gradually advances from simple single-celled organisms to simple plant life, insects, birds, and animals, becoming ever more complex until the emergence of a self-aware entity, which signals the entry into the Cycle of Self-Awareness. At this stage, the groundwork is laid not only to sustain the self-aware entity but also to grant it the opportunity to evolve, experience, and express itself.

To move forward, the self-aware entity must make a fundamental choice: to love and understand others or to love and understand the self—the way of the positive or the way of the negative, light or darkness. To love and understand others is to love one and all, while to love and understand the self is a more selfish and self-centered choice. This choice essentially dictates how a people and a planet will evolve through the remaining cycles up to the sixth—through the positive or the negative, the path of Light or Darkness.

Yes, we are here to live, experience the good and the bad, make mistakes, learn, and fulfill our desires to some extent, hopefully without becoming too karmically entangled. However, we eventually must move on from this and make our own fundamental choice. Know that the fate of a planet is directly intertwined with the choices of its people. Whatever choice is made, positive or negative, one can imagine two very different environments that reflect the nature of that choice.

Nonetheless, there are times when there is no definite direction toward one side or the other, resulting in a world of mixed nature. Our planet Earth is such an example; some are positive, others negative, and most stand in the middle, driven by passion and swinging from one side to the other. Most of us, despite the efforts of many, still ignore that there's even a choice to be made, while others choose to completely disregard it. In fact, the mixed nature of a planet is more conducive to impasse than choice.

Some of you may disagree and say that this planet is definitely of a negative nature. I know how you feel—I felt it too, for a very long time. However, this is not true. There are very good souls in this world, and others are well-established on a positive path, and you are very likely one of them. The problem is that darkness not only works in the shadows but also likes to take center stage, being loud and in-your-face. It moves to control and manipulate to keep us in place. In such a reality, it is indeed highly unlikely to expect any form of Heaven on Earth, but stay with the flow of this book, and you just might come to see a way.

Chapter Two
Law

Law is a system of rules created and enforced by social or governmental institutions to regulate behavior. It ensures order, resolves disputes, and protects liberties and rights. Laws are often codified in written statutes, but they can also emerge from customs, judicial decisions, and religious practices.

This is the textbook definition, which is of some use, but has its own limitations. Human law serves to control and direct human behavior; it usually reflects a society's ethical standards and sense of justice. Justice is a curious concept, as it flows and changes according to the minds in question. However, in a good-natured system, it will strive to balance individual rights with the common good.

Laws are more than instruments of order and justice; they are foundational to the functioning of society. They address a wide array of issues, from preventing crime to regulating various sectors such as government, industry, commerce, and labor. By determining modus operandi, laws establish what can and cannot be done, shaping the behavior of individuals and institutions alike.

Without the machinery of law enforcement—police, courts, regulatory agencies—no one would really care for it. It would have no effective power to shape behavior and ensure order. Enforcement is the backbone of any legal system. It transforms abstract rules into lived realities. When a law is enforced, it sends a clear message: compliance is not just expected but required. This deterrence prevents chaos, promoting safety and fairness.

Law in Worlds of Light and Darkness

There is a common misconception among the self-aware that the worlds of a negative nature are environments of chaos. This is not the case. There are indeed periods of chaos, but darkness soon puts things into proper order, or so they say. In its beginnings, it will start with a country, then pass to a continent and eventually a world. As darkness evolves, it will strive to put into order a star system, a galaxy, the universe. The principles mentioned above are, in essence, the same. What changes in systems of light and darkness is the nature of the law (positive or negative) and the hearts and minds of those who apply it.

Reflection on Crime and Society

I'm sure many of you expect me to address various forms of crime and come up with appropriate solutions to each of them. Sorry to disappoint, but I will not. Crime, like so many other issues, is just, in essence, a symptom of imperfect societies. We address these symptoms by creating and enforcing new laws, but this is like putting a bandage on a festering wound. Cutting off the diseased part will not resolve the underlying problem, and other issues will continue to emerge from the main body. The solution lies in creating a better society, which will lead many to say: Easier said than done. Yes, it will not be easy; nothing worth doing ever is, but follow the flow of this book and you just might change your mind in the end.

Chapter Three
<u>TRUTH: Culture – Tradition – Religion</u>

The Truth that I speak of is Universal Truth, not bound by Time or Space. There are Higher Truths, of course, but there are also various grades of it that have been conveyed in different ways to help the Self-Aware entity (man). My intention here is not to outline, or grade Truth in a systematic way, but rather to analyze a few, how they came to be, and how they found their place in the daily life's of different communities throughout human history. This light, general account aims to open the hearts and minds of many. Ultimately, I hope this exposition helps set humanity in the right tone to travel in a more harmonious path.

Truth is often conveyed through the scriptural texts of different religions. Islam, Christianity, Hinduism, Buddhism, Judaism, Sikhism, Taoism, and Zoroastrianism are just a few examples. The core Universal Truths present in all these religions are the same, yet these religious constructs seem so different to most of us, that they appear to be on opposing sides. Why is that? A few years ago, a metaphor came to me, and I believe it will help somewhat in the process of understanding.

The wheat that grows here and on the other side of the world might be called differently due to language, but it's wheat nonetheless. It comes to serve the same purpose. What

does happen, is that the soil might come to have different qualities that the plant will come to express, but what's planted is essentially the same.

Religions are shaped by the unique qualities of their respective cultures. Customs, traditions, and societal norms can shape the interpretations and practices within a religion. It's this diversity that gives rise to the rich tapestry of religious beliefs and rituals we see today. There is an underlying unity amongst all true religions, and yet we fail to see it, which in turn, more often than not, comes to put us in dire straits.

Let's try a different approach. Most people have a pretty fixed idea of Heaven. They determine that following a certain religion will lead them to the ultimate destination, the perfect place. You might be one of them. First of all, the idea of perfect varies as much as the people in question, but let's work with what we have. Take your time, and answer the following questions:

Do you think they teach religion in Heaven? If so, which one?

You do realize that Heaven existed long before any religion was established on Earth. Look, I'm not trying to antagonize anyone, and my exposition does have a point that will be made clear at the end.

Whatever the religion in question, we should all be thankful to the great souls that agreed to incarnate on Earth to convey

Universal Truth. This act of great love and compassion, allows the messenger to understand and empathize with the people of a certain time and culture, which in turn allows him to frame Truth in a more familiar fashion to the people in question. On the receiving end, the process makes the people more receptive to the message without seeing the messenger as a Godly figure, but this latter part does not always workout.

Devotees of different religions have a hard time understanding and accepting each other, but do realize that religion is a human construct, which in turn makes it imperfect. It could be said that some scriptural texts are more complete than others, but this more often than not works against them, ending up breeding confusion in the minds of many. The higher minds that came into this Earth envisioned helping in a certain way, and on this note, I would like to say that Buddha had a very curious outlook.

Buddhism is said to be a religion that does not believe in God, that puts its emphases in meditation and mindful living in order to achieve liberation from suffering. Now this idea of not putting God at the pivot of a certain path is quite out of a norm, but worth getting into. When asked about the nature of God and the Universe, the Buddha often remained silent. He would subsequently affirm that these questions were irrelevant to the path of liberation.

First of all, I would like to make clear that the liberation that the Buddha speaks of is ascending from a physical existence into a higher one, which in this case is Heaven. It is true that understanding God, Its Universal Laws and Creation is not a requirement to ascend from this plane of existence. Secondly, to say that Buddha didn't believe in God is somewhat of a stretch. He just knew that man was prone to putting himself in trouble, and thus, He crafted a path that focusses not on God but on the process. One should also realize that it would not be possible for Buddha to know, see and do what he did if he were not connected to the Infinite.

In Buddhism placing one's hearts and minds in the right place is of a fundamental importance, as it should be for the followers of every religion. Do not believe anything blindly; question, investigate and test the Truth for yourselves. The Ultimate Truth lies within ourselves and it can only be known by direct experience.

Well, one can go on and on about this topic, but let me get to the point, because all of this can become too cryptic for many to understand, and that is not my intention—quite the opposite. My point is this: maybe what we need to do in order to move forward as one is to simplify things. Humanity should reach a time and place where it teaches only goodness, kindness—Love—sprinkled with adequate amounts of wisdom unbound by politics, culture, tradition, religion, or anything else. The need for greater understanding may come, and if so, it will flourish within ourselves. But the starting point is this: Love.

Chapter Four
<u>Truth to Cultural Norm - Japan</u>

Even in this plane of existence, there are times when certain people become the living embodiment of a particular truth. In Japanese culture, this happened in a very natural, organic way, not by law or religious imposition. It sprouted from the individual's recognition that a certain thing is good and right, and as such, that something should be embraced and practiced in everyday life. Many people thinking and feeling the same way come to make it a cultural norm. There are exceptions to this, of course, as with everything else, but what's important to note is that this phenomenon springs from within, from the individual acknowledgment and embodiment of a certain truth. Japan is a very curious case, and it will serve as a prime example of the points I want to make.

The schools of thought that had the greatest influence on Japanese culture were Shintoism, Buddhism, and Confucianism. I refer to them as schools of thought because arguably, they are not religions in the conventional sense. Shintoism is a notable case because it did not originate from a single figurehead; instead, it evolved over a very long period. In fact, the origins of Shinto can be traced back to prehistoric Japan. Ancient animistic beliefs in spirits, known as kami, were integral to early Japanese societies. These spirits were believed to inhabit natural phenomena such as mountains, rivers, trees, and animals, as well as human ancestors. This system of belief came to be known as "Shinto" during the Nara period (710 to 794), in the later part of its evolutionary process, and only due to the need to distinguish it from the newly imported Buddhism. Shintoism is rich with an incredible amount of folklore, but there is truth within it as well.

What is good and right remains so, no matter its origin. It may come from philosophy, religion, or cultural tradition. The subjects I'm about to address are prime examples of this, and they usually come from a combination of these.

Work

The Japanese are renowned for their mindfulness and diligence in their work. This didn't happen overnight it evolved over several centuries, influenced by historical, social, cultural and economic factors.

In regards to the social and cultural influences that brought about this predisposition towards work, Confucianism played its part. The philosophy that emphasizes hierarchy, respect for authority, and the importance of the group over the individual, has deeply influenced Japanese culture. These values contribute to a work environment where employees are expected to show utmost dedication to their superiors and peers. This Confucian line of thought came to merge with a very crucial concept in Japanese society: "wa" or harmony. Maintaining harmony within the workplace means that employees often work extra hours to ensure that their team's goals are met and to avoid causing inconvenience to colleagues. In Japan, diligence and perseverance (gaman) are highly valued traits. The cultural emphasis on enduring hardship and striving for perfection permeates the work environment, encouraging employees to work diligently, often at the expense of their personal lives.

Historical Development

1. <u>Edo Period</u> (1603 to 1868)

- During the Edo period, the samurai class exemplified a strict code of conduct known as bushido, which emphasized loyalty, discipline, and honor. These values influenced the work ethic of not only the samurai but also the broader society. Merchants took some time to embrace these values for they seemed incompatible with their trade, but they eventually came to see them as good in the long run. This period laid the groundwork for a culture that valued hard work and dedication.

2. <u>Meiji Period</u> (1868 to 1912)

- The Meiji Restoration marked the beginning of Japan's rapid modernization and industrialization. The government promoted a work ethic that supported national development and industrial growth. Concepts such as "shokusan kogyo" (promote industry) and "fukoku kyohei" (rich country, strong army) were central to this period. Western ideas about work and organization began to be adopted, and the establishment of large conglomerates (zaibatsu) such as Mitsubishi and Mitsui further entrenched a culture of hard work and corporate loyalty.

3. Post-World War II Era

- After World War II, Japan's economy needed to be rebuilt. The government and companies promoted a collective effort to restore the nation. This period saw the rise of lifetime employment (shushin koyo) and seniority-based wage systems (nenko joretsu), which fostered loyalty and long-term dedication to a single company. The concept of "kaizen" (continuous improvement) became a cornerstone of Japanese business philosophy, encouraging constant self-improvement and efficiency in the workplace.

4. Economic Boom (1950s to 1980s)

- Japan's economic miracle during the 1950s to the 1980s saw unprecedented growth, leading to increased job security but also higher expectations for productivity and longer working hours. The term "karoshi" (death from overwork) emerged during this time, highlighting the severe consequences of the intense work culture. Company loyalty was paramount, and employees often worked long hours, participated in after-work social activities (nomikai), and prioritized company needs over personal life.

Separating The Good from the Bad

The diligence and mindfulness of the Japanese people is not exclusive to work, it touches all aspects of life, including the simplest of tasks. It comes from an individual acknowledgement that how you do anything, is how you do everything. Nothing should be done absentmindedly. I can relate to this state of being, but most people will not, they will label some things as more important that others, which in turn moves to control their actions, caring - doing more or less in accordance to whatever hierarchy they establish in their mind. However, this is a fickle state of being that is highly unreliable. What is important can change, and will change, in an instant. What happens then? Let's take a practical example.

The process of building a car involves numerous steps and components. To begin with, a variety of raw materials are required, including different types of plastics, rubbers, metals, glass, oils, and paints. These materials are used to create various car parts, many of which are outsourced to subcontractors rather than being manufactured in-house. Each car part undergoes several stages of development before it is completed. Once these parts are ready, they are brought together for the final assembly of the car.

This is a very simplified description, but it serves to make a point. What would you deem to be less important? The raw materials? A certain car part? Part of the process? The bolts, perhaps? Every little thing affects the overall quality and safety of the final product. Similarly, the diligent and mindful predisposition of people in all aspects of life will be reflected in the nature, caliber, and character of a society.

Many will label the Japanese as perfectionists, but that is not the case. They know, as most of us do, that perfection is not of this world. However, by striving to always do their best, they know that, over time, they will come to do better and better, no matter the task at hand.

Now, the overwork culture in Japan is a different matter entirely. This is a somewhat recent development and not a product of the values mentioned above. The original trigger for this was probably set by the end of World War II. Japan was devastated in more ways than one, and a global effort was needed to bring the country back from the ashes. The Japanese people responded in kind, and a generation sacrificed for the greater good. The commitment and resilience of the people led to the rise of the phoenix, and Japan saw incredible, unprecedented growth from the 1950s to the 1980s. The need for such a sacrifice was no longer present, but the culture of overwork continued to spiral down from bad to worse.

The Japanese people do not need my help to outline the problem, but they do seem helpless to escape it. In recent years, there have been efforts to address the negative aspects of overwork.

The Japanese government has implemented policies to promote work-life balance, such as the "Premium Friday" initiative, which encourages employees to leave work early on the last Friday of each month. Some companies are adopting more flexible work arrangements and promoting mental health and well-being initiatives to combat the culture of overwork. I'm sure that these seem like big moves when looking from within (for the Japanese), but these are feeble attempts to solve a very serious problem. Worst of all, those who suffer are grooming their children to go down that very same rabbit hole.

It pains me to see a country that prides itself on striving for harmony to lack in such a fundamental concept as balance. Having no balance within oneself breeds disharmony and hinders interpersonal relationships with family and friends, if you manage to have any. Japan has been paying the price for not addressing this problem seriously, and things will only get worse until they do so. I hope change can come soon, for it is for the benefit of all.

Respect

The deep-rooted respect that Japanese people show for one another has evolved over centuries, influenced by religious, philosophical, and cultural traditions. This respect is manifest in various social behaviors, including language, customs, and daily interactions. All languages have polite expressions, but the Japanese language came to develop an extensive system of honorifics used to express respect. Keigo has three main forms: sonkeigo (respectful language), kenjōgo (humble language), and teineigo (polite language). It is said to help maintain social harmony (wa) by acknowledging and respecting social hierarchies and relationships. Its use in daily interactions helps to define and reinforce social relationships, such as those between seniors and juniors (senpai-kōhai), employers and employees, and service providers and customers. Overall Keigo allows speakers to show respect, humility, and politeness, which are key values in Japanese culture.

Historical and Philosophical Roots

1. Confucian Influence

- Confucianism, which was introduced to Japan from China around the 6th century, significantly shaped Japanese social structures and interpersonal relationships. Confucian philosophy emphasizes respect for hierarchy, filial piety, and proper conduct within society.

2. Buddhist Influence

- Buddhism, also introduced in the 6th century, further reinforced values of respect, compassion, and mindfulness. Zen Buddhism, in particular, emphasized inner peace and harmony, which translated into respectful interactions with others.

3. <u>Shintoism</u>

- Shinto, the indigenous religion of Japan, places a strong emphasis on purity, harmony, and respect for nature and ancestors. Rituals and customs derived from Shinto practices promote reverence for all living things and respect for the natural world.

Social and Cultural Development

1. <u>Heian Period</u> (794 to 1185)

- During the Heian period, the aristocracy developed elaborate codes of etiquette that emphasized respect and proper conduct. Court life was governed by precise rules of behavior, reflecting a culture that valued politeness and consideration for others.

2. <u>Feudal Era</u> (1185 to 1868)

- The samurai class played a significant role in shaping Japanese values of respect and duty. The bushido (way of the warrior) code emphasized honor, loyalty, and respect for superiors and peers. These values permeated Japanese society, influencing not just the samurai but also common people.

- The Tea Ceremony (sadō): The tea ceremony, which became popular during the Muromachi period (1336 to 1573), epitomizes the principles of respect, harmony, and mindfulness. Here participants are expected to show utmost respect to the host, the tea utensils, and the other guests.

3. <u>Edo Period</u> (1603 to 1868)

- During the Edo period, Neo-Confucianism became the dominant ideology, further embedding Confucian values into Japanese society. This era saw the codification of social hierarchies and the establishment of norms that reinforced respect for authority, family, and community.

4. <u>Modern Era</u> (Meiji Period to Present)

- The Meiji Restoration (1868) and subsequent modernization efforts introduced Western influences, but traditional values of respect and social harmony remained central to Japanese culture. Education reforms in the Meiji period emphasized moral education (shūshin), which included lessons on respect and proper conduct.

- Contemporary Japan continues to value respect in social interactions, which is evident in the language, business etiquette, and daily customs. The importance of respect is taught from a young age and reinforced through societal norms and practices.

Reflections

I never thought that having respect, in a general sense, had any particular down side. However, I've seen that when taken to extremes it can make us miss opportunities to connect with one another. This may sound contradictory, but I believe that some will understand exactly what I mean. On the other hand, when we start talking about hierarchy, we unavoidably start to brand people as more and others less, which in turn leeds us to act with that thought in mind, and almost never in a positive way. Being respectful and polite is undoubtably a good thing, but we should never demean ourselves, nor should we do it to others. Conversely, respect and politeness should not make us oblivious to the true nature of any given interaction (positive or negative).

To finalize on this subject: respect and politeness are a natural reflection of a certain state of being, and not a product of adherence to a certain "protocol." It is true that these values should be nurtured from a very young age, but I put in to question the need for such strict protocols. These codes of conduct may come to vary greatly from culture to culture, but what one feels at heart never really changes.

In Japan there is an abundance of respect for a great deal of many things while in the west there seams to be a great lack of it, specially in our youth. Maybe we should come to meet them halfway, or more than halfway.

Cleanliness

Not Wearing Shoes Indoors

The habit of not wearing shoes indoors in Japan, a practice known as 'dosoku genkin,' has deep cultural and historical roots. While this custom is partly influenced by religious practices, it stems primarily from practical considerations, in other words, good common sense. The exact point where this practice originated may be lost, but its origin can be traced back to ancient Japan (Jomon and Yayoi periods). Early Japanese homes had dirt floors, and footwear, such as straw sandals (waraji) or wooden clogs (geta), were used primarily to navigate muddy or uneven terrain outside. As such, removing shoes before entering one's home was just the right thing to do. The Japanese people have an uncommon ability to incorporate a certain truth into their way of life; in this case, it was an early acknowledgment that "the greater the mess, the greater the cleanup." Well, this is at least part of it.

Religion came to reinforce this cultural practice. Both Shintoism and Buddhism emphasize purity and cleanliness. In Shinto, the act of removing shoes before entering a shrine or home is part of the broader practice of ritual purification. In Buddhism, removing shoes before entering a temple symbolizes respect for the sacred space, as it does in many other religions.

Over time, the practice continued to be reinforced. In the Heian period (794 to 1185), aristocratic homes began to feature raised wooden floors, which were more difficult to clean than dirt floors. Then, in the Kamakura and Muromachi periods (1185 to 1573), the samurai class adopted the custom of removing shoes to protect the tatami mats, which were becoming more widespread. This practice was also linked to the tea ceremony, where cleanliness and humility were emphasized. Finally, during the Edo period (1603 to 1868), removing shoes became a well-established practice among all social classes. Public bathhouses (sento) and private homes alike enforced this rule to maintain hygiene. The design of Japanese homes, with genkan (entrance areas) specifically for removing shoes, became standardized. This custom came to reinforce social norms of respect and humility, where entering someone's home without removing shoes is considered disrespectful and inconsiderate.

The habit of removing shoes continued into the modern era, reinforced by the introduction of Western-style footwear, which is less suited for indoor use. Japanese homes and public buildings maintained the genkan area for this purpose. Our human circumstances may change, but as we stand, humanity would benefit from making this practice a widespread phenomenon.

The Art of Cleaning and Tidying Up

The art of cleaning and tidying up can officially be traced back to 927 A.D. to a book called Engishiki. Among other things, it gave instructions for the annual cleaning of the Imperial Palace of Kyoto. This ritual was intended to sweep away a year's worth of ill fortune and evil spirits in anticipation of a fresh new start, effectively removing various agents of decay and their breeding grounds from one's home. With the aid of Shinto and Buddhist philosophies, housecleaning slowly began to spread to the overall populace. By the end of the seventeenth century, a great part of the

Japanese population was dedicating themselves to 'Oosouji,' which translates to 'big cleaning.' At the end of each year (December), each family would undertake a thorough cleaning of their homes, a tradition akin to spring cleaning in the West. In the modern age, this practice has been gradually fading away due to different household circumstances and the understanding that a house should be clean and uncluttered year-round.

Everyday Practices and Social Etiquette

In Japan, the art of cleaning extends beyond the home into public spaces. Streets, parks, and public transportation are remarkably clean, a testament to the collective responsibility ingrained in Japanese society. This is not enforced by law, but by social norms and a shared commitment to community well-being. Schools, for example, have "souji no jikan" (cleaning time), where students clean their classrooms and school grounds daily. This practice instills a sense of responsibility and respect for their environment from a young age. This predisposition comes to life from within, as the Japanese people see their home not just as their personal dwelling, but as their neighborhood, their city, their country, and their planet.

The Modern Manifestation: Marie Kondo and Beyond

In contemporary times, the Japanese art of tidying up has gained international acclaim, largely thanks to Marie Kondo and her KonMari method. Kondo's approach is not just about decluttering physical spaces, but also about creating an environment that nurtures joy and well-being. Her mantra, "Does it spark joy?" encourages individuals to mindfully evaluate their possessions, keeping only those items that truly enhance their lives.

Kondo's method is deeply rooted in Japanese cultural principles, such as "mottainai," a term expressing regret over waste, and "wabi-sabi," which finds beauty in imperfection and transience. By promoting gratitude for our belongings and a mindful approach to organization, Kondo has turned tidying up into a global phenomenon, resonating with people far beyond Japan.

I personally strive for a minimalist and practical approach, but at home, it feels like I'm pulling in one direction while everyone else pulls in another. Despite this fact, my home is still very different from the Western norm. This reminds me of a curious conversation I had with my wife. She was often nagging me to buy chandeliers for our home, and I often offered mild resistance to the idea, mostly because I was fond of having my lighting simple and effective. At one time, she asked if I had something against chandeliers, to which I replied: "No, I don't, but what's the point of such things that drain energy and buffer light? Much like most of our human lives. I don't have anything against chandeliers. However, if they do not focus on the primary purpose for which they were made, what is their worth?"

Bathing

The art of cleanliness naturally extended to the personal hygiene of the Japanese people. Regular bathing and washing have been significant parts of Japanese culture for centuries, in stark contrast to historical practices in many Western cultures. These practices have a clear religious influence, but they also stem from an early acknowledgment that regular bathing had many health benefits, such as the prevention of skin diseases, relaxation, and improved circulation.

Historically, evidence of ritual purification can be traced back to the Jomon period (14,000 to 300 BCE). The Yayoi period (300 BCE to 300 CE) saw the continuation and refinement of these practices. With the introduction of Buddhism from Korea and China in the 6th century, bathing practices were further influenced. Buddhist temples often included baths (yokudo), emphasizing the importance of personal cleanliness for spiritual reasons.

In the Heian Period (794 to 1185), the aristocratic elite placed a high value on personal hygiene and appearance, which led to the further refinement of bathing practices. This is not to say that the common people were not watchful of their personal hygiene. They might not have had the same conditions and opportunities, but they valued this practice and strived to maintain it to the best of their ability.

In the Kamakura and Muromachi periods (1185 to 1573), bathing became a more widespread phenomenon, partly due to the samurai class's influence. Public baths (sento) began to appear, offering a communal space for bathing. The Edo period (1603 to 1868) marked the height of public bathing culture. Public bathhouses became ubiquitous in urban centers, and the refined practice of bathing was no longer limited to the elite, as common people regularly visited bathhouses.

Western influences during the Meiji Restoration (1868 to 1912) led to further development of bathing facilities. Despite adopting some Western practices, the Japanese continued to emphasize cleanliness, integrating modern plumbing and sanitation technology.

Reflections

Many religions in the world emphasize the importance of pure water. The cleansing effects of pure water have been passed down through history in many religious traditions, which emphasize the importance of bathing and personal hygiene as daily practices. There are exceptions to this, and Christianity is one of them. It adheres to the idea of holy water that serves as a tool for the priestly caste. However, pure water is holy in itself and needs no sanctification.

In India, the act of bathing has been around since ancient times. The Rigveda, one of the oldest sacred texts, contains numerous hymns praising the purifying qualities of water. The practice of bathing in India is deeply intertwined with spiritual, cultural, and religious traditions. Bathing is not just a routine activity for personal hygiene; it is a ritual that holds profound significance, especially when it comes to the holy rivers of India. These rivers are considered sacred, and bathing in them is believed to purify the body, mind, and soul. Water indeed has such cleansing properties, and I mean clean, pure water. Let me explain as one who comes from a food safety and quality background.

The highest standard for water in the food industry is drinking water. I don't want to get overly technical, but this is too important to pass on, and there is a point here to be made. The quality indicators for drinking water are essential for ensuring it is safe for consumption. Here is an outline of key quality indicators:

Physical Indicators

1. **Color**: Water should be colorless. Any discoloration may indicate the presence of dissolved substances or contaminants.

2. **Turbidity**: This measures the clarity of water. High turbidity can indicate the presence of suspended solids, microorganisms, or organic matter.

3. **Taste and Odor**: Drinking water should be free from any unpleasant tastes or odors, which can indicate contamination by chemicals or biological agents.

4. **Temperature**: While not directly harmful, the temperature of water can affect its taste and the efficacy of treatment processes.

Chemical Indicators

1. **pH**: The pH level of drinking water should be between 6.5 and 8.5. This range ensures that the water is neither too acidic nor too alkaline. The Ideal is 7, and this is no random number.

2. **Dissolved Oxygen (DO)**: Adequate DO levels are necessary to maintain the taste, quality of water and to support aquatic life in water sources.

3. **Hardness**: Measured by the concentration of calcium and magnesium, water hardness affects taste and can lead to scaling in pipes.

4. **Total Dissolved Solids (TDS)**: TDS includes any minerals, salts, metals, and other dissolved substances in water. The recommended maximum level is typically 500 mg/L.

5. **Chemical Contaminants**: This includes nitrates, nitrites, heavy metals (like lead, arsenic, and mercury), pesticides, and volatile organic compounds (VOCs). These contaminants can pose serious health risks.

6. **Chlorine and Chloramine**: These are commonly used disinfectants. Their levels must be controlled to ensure effective disinfection without causing harmful effects.

Biological Indicators

1. **Coliform Bacteria**: The presence of coliform bacteria, especially Escherichia coli (E. coli), indicates potential contamination by fecal matter and the possible presence of pathogenic organisms.

2. **Pathogens**: This includes bacteria, viruses, protozoa, and helminths. Regular testing is essential to ensure these pathogens are absent.

3. **Biofilm**: The presence of biofilm can indicate bacterial growth in the distribution system, which can harbor pathogens.

Radiological Indicators

1. **Radon**: Radon is a naturally occurring radioactive gas that can dissolve in water and pose a health risk when ingested.

2. **Gross Alpha and Beta Activity**: These measure the total alpha and beta radiation in the water. Elevated levels can indicate contamination by radioactive substances.

Hindu scriptures speak a little of this, but far from such specific detail. The concept of holy rivers emphasizes the idea of the purity of their waters. However, many of these places have suffered greatly due to human presence, and the water is no longer clean or pure. In my trip to India, I remember seeing people bathing in the Ganges right outside Kali Temple. The waters were so heavily polluted that no scientific test or mind was needed to attest to the fact, but this didn't seem to affect them at all. I would not willingly bathe in such water, much less drink it. I mean not to shatter anyone's belief, but let no scripture or anything else make you blind to what is true.

We are so fortunate to have pure, clean water to bathe and drink. Many places on Earth are not so fortunate. In some areas, drinking water is scarce and must be carefully managed; in others, there's none to be had. We should treasure and preserve what we have, always remembering never to be wasteful.

Conclusion

Japanese society is not perfect, of course, but it is rare to see a people embrace a certain truth and turn it into a cultural norm. Mind you that this is not forced, it has a beautiful, organic flow that begins at a personal level to be reflected in a society. We get hung up in so many things that hold us back, many are troublesome, not particularly good or helpful, but still, we resist and persist. I'm not really one for quotes, but Buddhas words are right on the money.

"When you know for yourselves that certain things are unwholesome and wrong, then give them up, and when you know for yourselves that certain things are wholesome and good, then accept them and follow them." (Aṅguttara Nikāya 3.65)

Chapter Five

Offerings and Sacrifice

When a self-aware entity comes into existence, it begins to roam the world to find its place, encountering both good fortune and misfortune. Soon, it realizes that not much is within its control. Still young and lacking in understanding, it acknowledges the presence of greater forces at work. With this thought, it turns to the One God or to divine entities, praying and making offerings to seek favor: a good harvest, a successful hunt, good health, protection, fertility, and overall good fortune. Initially, it presents gifts of value such as grain, fruit, drink, flowers, etc. These offerings may vary but usually fall within the same category.

This simple act of seeking favor is natural and understandable for the self-aware entity. However, this line of reasoning is flawed. You are essentially giving back what was already His. On the other hand, you toil greatly to take from an ocean and then seek favor by giving back a pint. This seems like the reasoning of a special kind of thief. You would do a far better service to the One you aim to please by providing for those in need.

There often comes a time when those making offerings realize that something is not working. They reason that a greater offering is needed to please and appease. As a result, they either increase the size of their previous offerings or offer something of greater value, often an animal sacrifice. Not all self-aware entities reach this point, but those with a violent propensity certainly do, and mankind is no exception. We may be dull to many things, but we do seem to maintain the ability to recognize higher expressions of life.

Beyond this point, it's easy to find circumstances where the sacrifice of a self-aware entity appears justified. This unfortunate state of affairs has happened many times and continues to happen. The Universal Creation has a natural distaste for blood; many of us can feel it, but many others choose to act otherwise for various reasons. I realize that sometimes this choice results from faulty reasoning birthed within ourselves or imposed by others, so I will explain using our little corner of creation.

God toiled for billions of years to bring about our cradle of life. Our star system, like many others, has a limited number of celestial bodies with the potential to create life, and not all of those can sustain and nurture the growth of a self-aware entity. These spheres have to be nurtured with great care over a very long period to bring about a self-aware entity, which in our case is humanity. With that said, let me ask you this: Do you think that God went to all this trouble to create you so that you could sacrifice and kill in His name?

Personal Sacrifice

Personal sacrifice can be a variation of what I mentioned above. The self-aware entity knows and understands pain and suffering all too well. It is a difficult state of being that can easily be seen as a way of seeking favor or doing penance. This line of reasoning may lead many to put themselves through extreme situations. However, what we fail to understand is that the Divine does not want or care for these things. Jesus Christ said, "*I desire mercy, not sacrifice*" (Matthew 9:13), and so did the prophet Hosea: "*God desires mercy, not sacrifice.*" Many true religions have tried to convey this idea in one way or another, but we tend to resist and ignore it.

Now, sacrificing oneself for another is an entirely different matter, as it doesn't stem from selfish self-interest. It is an expression of love very close to our hearts, a language we can easily understand, and Jesus Christ exemplified it well. Many say that Jesus died to carry and atone for "our sins," but this is not true; no one soul can or should carry the "sins" of the world. Each soul is responsible for itself and will bear the weight of cause and effect, for good or ill. Some loving souls may help us in our process but not to take the burden of responsibility from us, and certainly not for an entire planet. This idea, while flawed, did inspire many, and as such, I consider it to be good.

Jesus's death conveyed the last, and perhaps one of the most important messages of his life. Jesus came to show forgiveness in its highest form. Not only did he have true forgiveness in his heart, but he also pleaded forgiveness for others when he said, "*Father, forgive them; for they know not what they do.*" (Luke 23:34).

There will be plenty of people who do you "wrong" in this life, but how many of you find true forgiveness within yourselves? Mankind should take a cue from this example if we are to move forward as a whole, but never forget to be wise in this endeavor.

Chapter Six
Forms of Governance

Governance is the framework through which societies are managed, encompassing the structures and processes that ensure stability, order, and direction in a community. Throughout history, various forms of governance have evolved, each reflecting the unique cultural, economic, and philosophical contexts of their times. It would be challenging to delve into the intricacies of each system and their variations in detail. Therefore, I will speak in a general sense. They may be lacking in many ways, but they will serve as a background for the points I want to make. Here are some examples:

1. Monarchy

Monarchy is one of the oldest forms of governance, characterized by the rule of a single person—typically a king or queen—who holds power for life. This form can be absolute, where the monarch has almost complete control, or constitutional, where their powers are restricted by law or a governing body. Monarchies have been central to the development of many of the world's great civilizations, from ancient Egypt to medieval Europe. Modern constitutional monarchies, such as those in the United Kingdom and Japan, blend traditional royal elements with democratic processes.

2. Democracy

Democracy, derived from the Greek words "demos" (people) and "kratos" (power), is a system where power is vested in the people. It can take various forms, including direct democracy, where citizens vote on laws and policies directly, and representative democracy, where they elect representatives to make decisions on their behalf. Ancient Athens is often cited as the birthplace of democracy, though modern democracies are more complex, with intricate systems of checks and balances to prevent the abuse of power.

3. Oligarchy

Oligarchy is a form of governance where power rests with a small, elite segment of society, often distinguished by nobility, wealth, family ties, or military control. This system can be seen in the Spartan society of ancient Greece, where a few powerful families dominated political decision-making. While oligarchies can be efficient, they often lead to social inequality and can be resistant to change, as the ruling elite seeks to maintain its power and privileges.

4. Theocracy

Theocracy is governance by religious leaders, where the state is seen as divinely guided, and religious law is paramount. Ancient Egypt and Tibet under the Dalai Lamas are historical examples. In a theocracy, political leaders are often religious leaders, and policies are heavily influenced by religious doctrines. Modern examples include Iran, where Islamic law plays a central role in governance, and Vatican City, governed by the Pope according to Catholic principles.

5. Totalitarianism

Totalitarianism is an extreme form of authoritarianism where the state seeks to control nearly every aspect of public and private life. It often involves a single leader or party with absolute power, utilizing propaganda, surveillance, and state terror to maintain control. Notable examples include Nazi Germany under Adolf Hitler and the Soviet Union under Joseph Stalin. These regimes are characterized by their suppression of dissent, centralized control of the economy, and the use of extensive state propaganda to manipulate and control the populace.

6. Federalism

Federalism is a system where power is divided between a central authority and various constituent regions or states. This structure allows for a balance of power, enabling regions to maintain their own governance while contributing to the central government. The United States is a prime example, with its division of powers between federal, state, and local governments. Federalism promotes regional autonomy while ensuring a unified national policy.

7. Republic

A republic is a form of governance where the country is considered a "public matter" (res publica), and the head of state is an elected or nominated president, not a monarch. Power rests with elected individuals representing the citizen body and government leaders must follow the rule of law. The Roman Republic is one of the earliest examples, where a complex system of checks and balances was employed to prevent any single individual from gaining too much power. Modern republics include the United States, France, and India, each with their own unique systems of governance.

8. Anarchy

Anarchy refers to the absence of a governing body or authority. While often associated with chaos and disorder, philosophical anarchism advocates for self-managed, stateless societies based on voluntary cooperation. Anarchist thinkers like Peter Kropotkin and Emma Goldman envisioned societies where people govern themselves through decentralized, non-hierarchical structures.

Do They Make a Difference

There was an author, whose name I can't remember, who said that the form of governance doesn't matter as long as those who govern are of good nature. That is absolute nonsense. It's selling you a lie by telling half-truths. It is true that in our human history, kings, pharaohs, and other entitled leaders have brought forth great periods of human development, both spiritual and material. Some did come to recognize that their position was not one of birthright but a responsibility that only those of a specific character should inherit. Notwithstanding, darkness is sure to follow where there is light, whether by birthright or force. Once a dark pattern is established, it's almost impossible to break free, at least not without paying a high price.

The primary purpose of a system of governance is to serve the people and not the other way around, especially if that system is channeled to benefit the interests of a few. Acknowledgment of this fact may lead you to see that certain forms of government will be more conducive than others in maintaining the status quo of a few. There are, of course, no perfect systems to apply in a world of such mixed nature, but democracy may come to ensure that darkness does not linger for too long. Well, this is what I would like to believe to be true, but things have gotten increasingly more complex. Let me explain a little by addressing a few points.

Mixed World

In my previous book, I shared the insight I was given about the current numbers for this mixed-natured world. To recap, in the year 2020, 30% of those who are born are of a positive nature, equaled in the same by those of a negative one; the rest (40%) dwell in the middle, swinging like the wind to one side or the other. Well, this last part is not exactly true because it's easier to pull us into darkness than the other way around, and in an elective democratic system, this is not a point to be dismissed.

First, let me say that these are global numbers, not specific to any country. Secondly, these numbers may be higher in the extremes from what they were 20 or 40 years ago, but the balance between positive and negative is the same. With that said, let's consider the important part.

We must acknowledge that we are pretty easily riled up, and under certain circumstances, those of a negative predisposition will seek to gain power by taking advantage of this fact. By calling to fear and anger, they will easily sway 50% of the populace, and if some desire is mixed into the pot, these numbers will go way beyond that. Now, whether these are voters or not is another question, but those on the positive side should be mindful of this fact and address certain subjects wisely.

<u>Agendas</u>

Those of a negative nature will always strive to acquire positions of power. Politics is just another playground where they will do whatever they can to get ahead. As such, a certain game is played to push through one's own self-interest. Positive entities, on the other hand, care not for positions of power, but some do feel a duty to make the world a better place. Notwithstanding, by venturing to make a difference through politics, you will see yourself playing a game that will inadvertently change you. So many agendas will come into play, and you may come to forget why you were there in the first place.

We seem to live in the midst of a negative game, and not just in politics. At times, this seems like the only game being played, and as long as there are those who are willing to play it and feed it, nothing will really change. Those of a negative nature are all too willing to play it, while all others may come to feed it for a number of reasons. Many will think that they have no choice, some may feel that in time their efforts will be acknowledged, while others endure for the sake of a certain goal. However, this state of affairs will in time take its toll on one's soul, well at least on positive ones. Mind you, I'm not telling you what to do. Do as thou wilt. Every person and circumstance is unique, and we all have our own choices to make. I just strive to frame things in a certain light so that others may see more clearly. Notwithstanding, I would like to say that things will be exponentially more difficult to bear once you take conscious awareness of what's being done. In this world, this seems to be an enduring game, but at the very least, we should strive to find ways of feeding it a little less.

Perception (Media)

Public perception has always been a delicate and manipulable entity, influenced by the voices that shout the loudest and the narratives that seem the most convincing. Historically, control over public perception was wielded through newspapers, radio, and television—media that required significant resources to influence, thus limiting the number of players who could effectively shape public opinion. However, in our digital age, this dynamic has shifted dramatically. The advent of video and audio manipulation technologies, coupled with the pervasive influence of social media, has propelled the art of manipulating public perception to unprecedented levels of sophistication and reach. Alarmingly, even mainstream media, once considered bastions of reliability, are not immune to these influences.

The Power of Digital Manipulation

Digital manipulation technologies have evolved to the point where creating realistic but entirely fabricated video and audio content is within reach of anyone with a computer and the necessary software. Deepfakes, which use artificial intelligence to create hyper-realistic videos of people saying or doing things they never actually did, have become increasingly common. These can be weaponized for political disinformation, character assassination, or creating social unrest. For instance, a deepfake video of a political leader making inflammatory statements could spark violence or sway election outcomes.

Similarly, audio manipulation can create fake recordings that are nearly indistinguishable from genuine ones, further blurring the lines between reality and fabrication. These tools undermine trust, as people become uncertain about the authenticity of the media they consume.

The Influence of Social Media

Social media platforms have democratized the dissemination of information, allowing anyone to broadcast their message to a global audience. While this has many positive aspects, it also means that misinformation and manipulative content can spread rapidly and widely. Algorithms designed to maximize engagement often prioritize sensational and emotionally charged content, regardless of its truthfulness. This creates echo chambers where misinformation is amplified, and alternative viewpoints are suppressed.

Moreover, social media can be used to conduct sophisticated influence campaigns. Bot accounts and troll farms can flood platforms with coordinated messages, creating the illusion of widespread consensus or dissent. Hashtags can be hijacked, and trending topics can be manipulated to push specific agendas. The anonymity of the internet also allows bad actors to operate with impunity, further complicating efforts to maintain the integrity of public discourse.

The Erosion of Trust in Mainstream Media

In this environment, even mainstream media outlets, which have traditionally been seen as gatekeepers of truth, are not beyond reproach. The race for clicks and views has driven some outlets to prioritize sensationalism over rigorous journalism. This, combined with instances of biased reporting and the occasional propagation of false information, has eroded public trust. As people become more skeptical of the media, they are more susceptible to alternative sources of information, which may be less reliable.

Furthermore, the polarization of media outlets, where certain news channels are seen as catering to specific political ideologies, has led to a fragmentation of public perception. Individuals are increasingly consuming news that reinforces their existing beliefs, creating divided realities where people cannot even agree on basic facts.

Failing Checks and Balances

In the text above I identify the United States, France, and India as modern republics. This may lead some in to confusion, for many see them as democracies, which they are. One does not exclude the other, and these are example of democracies that incorporate republican principles, where elected representatives govern according to laws that protect individual rights and the public good.

The concept of checks and balances is fundamental to preventing the concentration of power in a single individual or group within a republic. Lets take the United States of America as an example. The U.S. Constitution establishes a federal system with a clear separation of powers among three branches of government: the Executive, Legislative, and Judicial.

Executive Branch: The President has the power to veto legislation passed by Congress, appoint federal judges (with Senate approval), and act as Commander-in-Chief of the armed forces.

Legislative Branch: Congress, comprising the Senate and the House of Representatives, can pass laws, override presidential vetoes with a two-thirds majority, approve federal budgets, and impeach and remove the President and federal judges.

Judicial Branch: The Supreme Court and lower federal courts can interpret laws and declare acts of Congress or executive actions unconstitutional through judicial review.

These checks and balances are good and right, and many democracies have them. However, I would advise against being overconfident. A system is made of people, and considering the above-mentioned to be true, given time and opportunity, the wrong people will weave their ways into its various parts, which will ultimately lead to dire consequences. Another factor to consider is the size of the beast—in other words, the size of the system at play. Motivations aside, it may be too great to ensure proper oversight.

Chapter Seven
The Migration Problem

This is one of the pressing matters in today's society, and it serves as an example of subjects that should be addressed wisely. "Problem" is a curious label to put on such natural phenomena, but I will endeavor to share my thoughts. We should first recognize that we are dealing with very limiting factors. The first ones are the concepts of border and country. These concepts are very much alive in the minds of men, and if not for them, we would see people exactly for what they are – people. The second limiting factor is the minds of those who migrate and the melting pot that makes up the country that receives them. We live in a world that does not grant the luxury of ignoring these facts. As such, the phenomenon called migration can indeed be a problem, a very complex one with no perfect solution.

To those who seek to migrate, I would advise you not only to abide by the laws in place but also to understand and respect the people, culture, tradition, and religion at play. This might not guarantee success, whatever that might be, but it will certainly be the right predisposition on your part. If you don't like a country's culture, religion, or general predisposition, why go there in the first place?

Ill feelings will inadvertently arise in the people of a country that receives a big wave of migration. Even good people will have a tendency to feel overwhelmed. Feelings of being invaded from within may come to touch the minds of many, which, when coupled with a sense of abuse of one's hospitality, will definitely come to breed trouble.

Unqualified Labor

The general populace often feels that these migrants come to take their jobs, but in a fair, law-abiding social economy, this does not happen, at least in regards to unqualified labor. The general reality is that the jobs that get taken are those that national citizens are often unwilling to do. In regards to qualified labor, we have a different story entirely, and I would like to give some examples very close to home.

Qualified Labor

In my country, for reasons that I cannot really fathom, there is a shortage of medical doctors. Due to the unwillingness of whoever is in power to address this issue, there comes the need to employ doctors from other countries. This is a rightful act that results from an unfortunate state of things.

Contrary to medical doctors, we have an overabundance of dentists in multiple fields, but despite this fact, many foreign workers are granted access to our national market. Worse still, many of them use our country as a point of access to the rest of Europe, which in turn breeds discontentment in many EU members. If these qualified workers were to open a clinic of their own, this would be a different matter, but the market is already overly saturated. There are more dental clinics than coffee shops, and believe me, we do have a lot of them.

Abuse

Migration and the provision of social services, such as child benefits, have become increasingly contentious issues in Europe. While many European countries pride themselves on robust social safety nets designed to support all residents, including migrants, there is growing discontent among native populations regarding the perceived abuse of these systems.

Child benefits, also known as family allowances, are crucial in assisting families with the costs of raising children. These benefits vary significantly across Europe. In my country there's no way one can survive on child benefits, no matter how many kids you have. However, in some northern European countries, the sums granted per child are more mindful, reflecting these countries' broader social welfare policies.

The contention arises from the perception that migrants are disproportionately benefiting from these generous social services. Critics argue that some migrant families have larger numbers of children, leading to substantial payouts from the state. This perception fuels resentment among native populations who believe that their tax contributions are being unfairly utilized to support migrant families. I would like to point out that there are national citizens that do the very same thing, but we do get angrier when we see "outsiders" doing it. When something is "wrong," it is so for all. If a system is being abused, then the system must change and adapt, no need to get angry about it.

It is crucial to balance the legitimate concerns of native populations with a fair and humane approach to migrant welfare. The subject of migration is only one of many that sprout from the complexities of the human mind and the imperfect systems at play. As things stand, there are no perfect solutions, but things might change, and you might come to see it by the end of this book.

Chapter Eight
Currency (Money)

There are some words that were spoken to me in India that I would like to call to attention, for they had an ultimate purpose which will be made clear at the end of this exposition. In a very curious event, an old renunciant conveyed these words:

"God and Guru say that money is impure..."

This reference to money stuck with me, but in my book, I said, and rightly so, that things were not that simple. To better understand all this, lets take a look of how currency came to evolve over time, and how it played a role in the development of a system and certain concepts.

Currency And Its History

The exchange system is the basis of the economy, but currency was not always an integral and fundamental factor. When it did not exist, there was direct exchange of goods and services, where something owned was exchanged for something desired, requiring mutual interest from both parties. Often, this mutual desire was not met, leading to the necessity of multiple exchanges before achieving the desired objective. Additionally, issues of fairness in terms of value, whether in relation to goods or services, further complicated these exchanges. To address these problems, local markets were created where exchanges took place with predetermined relative values. However, this method only partially solved the issue.

The Birth of Currency

To solve the problem of direct exchanges, some societies identified items of general acceptability and value that could be used in trade. Bread is a good example of such a general utility good. It was used as a form of payment because it was valued by everyone. This marked the birth of "currency," although it was not in the format we recognize today. Throughout history, various goods like bread, wine, and livestock were used as currency. However, these goods had non-monetary uses and were often consumed, leading to currency shortages.

For instance, if bread was used as currency and consumed, the person no longer had anything to exchange. Additionally, bread would spoil if stored, losing its usefulness and value.

The First Coins

This dilemma was resolved with the use of decorative or luxury goods, such as shells, pearls, diamonds, and precious metals, where non-monetary consumption was minimal. These goods were generally valued and accepted by everyone, but only some could properly perform the function of exchange currency. They needed specific characteristics:

- **Divisibility:** To facilitate exchanges and ensure that payments could be made for goods of varying values.

- **Durability:** Unlike perishable goods, the currency needed to maintain its value over time.

- **General Acceptability:** The currency had to be recognized and valued by everyone.

- **Reduced Non-Monetary Demand:** To avoid fluctuations in the amount of currency available.

- **Value Maintenance:** The assigned value had to be stable to facilitate transactions.

- **Convenient Transport:** Practical to move, avoiding excessive volume and weight.

- **Difficulty to Falsify:** To prevent fraud.

Precious metals like gold and silver met these criteria. Despite their weight, they were highly valued and small quantities held significant value, making authenticity verification relatively easy. This led to the use of heavy currency, where exchanges were based on the weight of gold or silver.

To streamline this process, gold and silver balls and discs with predetermined weights were created. These were authenticated by authorities like emperors or kings, who placed their seal on the coins, giving rise to minted coins with standardized weights and values.

The Evolution of Currency and New Concepts

Internationally, few currencies had general validity, complicating transactions between regions. Money changers emerged to buy and exchange currencies. Often goldsmiths, these money changers also rented safes to store customers' currency, issuing receipts for deposits. These receipts, worth the same as the deposited gold, became a precursor to paper currency. Eventually, standardized receipts were issued, functioning as currency and leading to the birth of banks.

As receipts circulated and gold remained largely untouched, money changers began lending gold, charging interest. This led to issuing more receipts than there was gold, a practice that could lead to bankruptcy if all receipts were redeemed simultaneously. Government intervention eventually led to states taking over currency issuance, creating paper currency backed by law, not gold.

This fiat currency was accepted due to trust in the system, resolving issues of finding a suitable exchange good. Currency became directly linked to inflation: as demand for goods increased, their value rose, causing currency to lose value.

Bank Resistance and New Forms of Currency

Despite losing the lucrative business of issuing currency, banks adapted by accepting state-imposed currency, continuing to pay interest on deposits and lending money. Various credit types emerged, always favorable to lenders, though banks could still go bankrupt. Banks also facilitated money transfers and issued checks, introducing scriptural currency.

New types of currency continue to emerge, with physical currency used less frequently. Alongside credit and debit cards, digital options like cryptocurrencies, digital wallets, and tokens have become prevalent.

Thoughts and Reflections

The evolution of currency to modern money was a natural process and has been a fundamental factor in social systems and the development of new structures. However, money has become the focus of our desire, with its promise of fulfilling all others. Money itself is not inherently good or bad; it is what we make it. Unfortunately, it has become just another instrument of control. At this point, this seems like an inescapable reality, as we need it to satisfy our most fundamental needs. We've been driven into a system that leads us to earn more, to spend more, to have more. Mind you, this is only true for a few; for most of us, it's earn more, to spend more, and have the exact same thing, or less. Money has played its role in the history of mankind, but if we want to move forward to a better place, maybe we should start to move past it.

Chapter Nine

<u>Inequality</u>

You might have inquired at some point in your life about the reasons for so much inequality in this world. My first book, as well as the flow of this one, may have made the reasons self-evident, but I'll endeavor to explain even more by resorting to a story. A woman belonging to a somewhat privileged social class came for a visit. She was telling my wife how annoyed she was after an encounter with a woman who reproached her for going on strike so often.

The Woman: **"Don't you feel bad for complaining when you have so much and others have so little?"**

My Visitor: **"No, I don't. If they are in such a bad situation, they should fight for their rights as I'm doing for mine."**

Immediately after hearing this, a thought flowed into my mind: "*I understand. You just want more.*" I didn't say it out loud because my words would only fuel conflict, not change. What my visitor failed to understand, or cared not to, was that few have the social and economic standing to "fight" as she does. The reality for many is that if you don't work, you don't eat.

From here, two issues come to light. First, we live in a world where we grade people by class. Some are more and others are less. The second issue is that as long as someone wants more, whether driven by fear or desire, there will always be another who ends up on the short end of the stick. We are entities with very few needs, but we appear to have many wants. The woman who came to visit is not a bad person; she just inherited what seems to be a very common mindset. On the other hand, these issues are not specific to a particular class; they branch out to all people in all walks of life. This world feeds and encourages this state of being. Change is possible, but it still seems so very far from us.

Chapter Ten
Strange and Unprecedented Growth

The rapid growth and unprecedented evolution of humankind began roughly 500 years ago, with a series of transformative developments that set the stage for the modern era. This period saw profound changes that collectively paved the way for the rapid advancements we witness today.

The Agricultural Revolution of the 18th century marked a significant shift from traditional farming methods to more productive agricultural practices. Innovations such as crop rotation, selective breeding, and new tools increased food production, supporting population growth and freeing up labor for other sectors.

The Scientific Revolution, spanning the 16th and 17th centuries, revolutionized human understanding of the natural world. Figures like Galileo, Newton, and Kepler made groundbreaking discoveries in physics, astronomy, and mathematics. These advancements laid the intellectual groundwork for technological innovation and industrial application.

The Enlightenment of the 18th century further accelerated human progress by promoting reason, individualism, and scientific inquiry. Philosophers like Voltaire, Rousseau, and Kant challenged traditional authority and advocated for knowledge based on empirical evidence and rational thought.

The Commercial Revolution, beginning in the late medieval period and continuing into the early modern era, transformed economies through the expansion of trade, the establishment of joint-stock companies, and the development of financial institutions. This period of economic dynamism created a more interconnected and prosperous world, facilitating the flow of goods, capital, and ideas.

Pre-industrial Inventions provided essential technological foundations. Innovations like the water wheel, the spinning wheel, and advancements in metallurgy were critical in developing the tools and machines that would later drive industrial production.

European Colonial Expansion from the 16th to the 18th centuries played a crucial role in accumulating capital, accessing new resources, and establishing global trade networks. These factors were instrumental in fueling industrial and economic growth.

The culmination of these developments was the **Industrial Revolution**, beginning in the late 18th century. It brought about the mechanization of production, the rise of factories, and significant technological innovations such as the steam engine, the power loom, and the cotton gin. These advancements revolutionized manufacturing, transportation, and communication.

In the 20th century, the **Digital Revolution** marked another transformative period, driven by the advent of computers, the internet, and digital communication technologies. This revolution has continued to evolve, leading to the current era of artificial intelligence, biotechnology, and advanced materials science.

Today, humanity stands at the forefront of an era characterized by rapid technological advancement and unprecedented interconnectedness. Innovations in fields such as quantum computing, renewable energy, and space exploration hold the promise of further transforming our world. The foundations laid over the past 500 years have enabled a trajectory of growth and development that continues to accelerate, shaping a future of limitless possibilities.

Some Disclosure

I apologize for being descriptive of certain subjects and concepts. I like to be clear and concise, but I do have to acknowledge that a certain background has to be laid before explaining a certain thing.

How did we come to evolve so much, and in such a short amount of time? It seems like only yesterday we were playing in the dirt. You do realize that mankind has been around for tens of thousands of years, and we never seemed to get anywhere. I could actually give you a number on this, but it would serve no one. What's important to note is that this was a strange and surprising turn of events, and as such, we should question how this happened and why.

It may surprise you to know, or not, that a Divine Plan has been at play. It was forged and put into action more than two thousand years ago, and part of that plan was putting in place the steps mentioned above. This was, and is, quite a Grand Plan, and I don't have full disclosure on it, but I will share what I can. A big part of this plan was banking on our greed to bring humanity here, and if there is something that can be consistently relied on, that something is certainly human greed.

In the last 25,000 years, there have been other attempts to help mankind. Some of these have been scantily recorded in history, like the Mayans and the Egyptians (**See Appendix One**). Others have fallen into myth and little is known for certain. Whatever the case, be sure to know that these were meant to be beacons of light for the rest of the world. However, these attempts over time ended up in "failure" due to one very simple reason: they relied on human kindness and goodness to succeed. It may seem like a harsh judgment, but in a world of mixed nature, light will not linger long without various attempts to put it out.

Mankind has been struggling greatly to move forward since its coming into this world. We are intelligent creatures, but we seem to lack the wisdom to keep moving forward. In fact, we seemed to be stuck in a continuous loop, moving back and forth. To aid mankind, many good souls came willingly into this world to play a number of different roles. Many came to convey knowledge, often scientific or technical, moving humanity closer to where it should be. Of course, this knowledge always ended up being manipulated for the greater profit of the few, but it ultimately led to the overall development of the world.

So why did this plan succeed in bringing about such material development? The answer is simple, and it's not greed—well, not in itself. This part of the Divine Plan played well with the negative agenda, as the number and variety of opportunities to turn and polarize entities further would increase almost exponentially. Greed did indeed bring us here, but it did so imperfectly and dangerously.

In an overpopulated world with limited resources, where most of us strive to have it all, what do you think will inadvertently happen? I don't want to sound ominous, but a very tight balance is being kept, and it can fall in an instant. We have little to no love for each other; we'll easily kill and eat each other up. Highly populated centers are prime powder kegs, but it will easily spread out to other populated centers. We have a very fundamental choice to make. Many ignore it, and others disregard it, but if you don't move to make it, a choice just might be made for you.

Now, this plan may only seem to be serving a negative purpose, but I assure you it is not. Firstly, you have to realize that the mixed nature of this world has long been established, and as such, we had to work with what we have. Secondly, light has been working greatly to raise the overall consciousness of men, which hasn't been easy. A great many things, big and small, have been put to work. Some of them I do not fully agree with, but if they come to help even just a little, I consider them good. On the other hand, the overall development of mankind will come to grant the opportunity for humanity to change as a whole.

Chapter Eleven
<u>How to Go About It</u>

What I will propose can bring about root change of planetary proportion, for it aims to create a system that nurtures and feeds another kind of human predisposition. So how do we, as a people, go about promoting this radical change? Well, the answer is simple, not easy, but simple.

By eradicating fear and desire.

Easier said than done, I know, but stay with me. Fear and desire are deeply woven into our human nature. They shape our perceptions, drive our actions, and influence our interactions with the world around us, but almost never in a positive way. It is, of course, impossible to completely eradicate fear and desire from this plane of existence. This will come much, much later at the end of a very Universal Process. Notwithstanding, it is possible to create a society where these are greatly diminished. I will start with its fundamentals and elaborate later on to whatever measure I am allowed to.

Satisfying Basic Human Needs

A global society must come to satisfy the most basic needs of its people, and it must do it for FREE. It is said that our most basic needs are food, water, air, and shelter. If any one of these basic needs is not met, then humans cannot survive. Seeing that mankind has come a long way, I will strive to expand somewhat on these basic needs.

1. **The need for adequate food and clean water (See Appendix Two).**

2. **The need for proper shelter.** This will mean different things depending on what circumstance humanity finds itself in, but here are some points:

    - A minimalistic dwelling, comfortable, practical, functional, and uncluttered, of sufficient size to accommodate those living in it;

    - It should be a wholesome environment of stable temperature, humidity, clean airflow, and adequate natural/artificial lighting;

    - Adequate structures for one to eat, sleep, and relax;

    - Means to attend to one's hygiene and maintain the wholesomeness of one's dwelling.

3. **The need for adequate indoor and outdoor clothing.**

4. **The need to feel safe in one's home, city, and planet.**

Restrain Desire

In this society, no one would be allowed to hoard and manipulate resources for one's own benefit, much less to exert control over others. What you can have will be pretty much standard. Those who contribute more will be granted a little more, and here I do mean a little. What this will be will depend on our current human circumstance, and it would be unwise of me to say this or that, but whatever it might be, it would never be something worth fighting for.

At this point, we should come to realize that we are all in each other's service. Our capacity to serve in this society will vary in accordance with one's ability and predisposition, but that will not make you more than any other. We are all important instruments of the same, and embodying the proper frame of heart and mind will come to be reflected in the society as a whole.

For example: If you are chosen to be a healer, it's because you have the ability and right predisposition to do so, and not just because you want to. Your "desire" to serve in a certain manner will always be taken into account, but you would never be allowed to be in a position you're not able to properly fulfill, and this goes far beyond know-how. There may still be promotions in certain fields, but these will be gained on merit after very careful consideration, and these may not entitle you to anything more.

This society will be very attentive to its children, nurturing and guiding them properly. There will be general teachings, of course, but once a certain propensity is acknowledged, steps will be taken to nurture it over time. At a certain point, you might be guided to follow in a certain direction, but you may choose to follow a different path. The same applies when you are offered a certain position; you may choose to try something else, although there is no guarantee of getting there. In a similar way, in time you may feel the need to strive for a different form of service than the one you are in, and you are free to pursue it. Whatever the case may be, you will not be bound by fear or the ideas of others, just as long as you abide in good nature.

There will be many worthy pursuits in this world. I would say that every service that is done in the right spirit will be a worthy one, but there may be those who choose to do nothing. Yes, this will certainly be a possibility, but it will be greatly frowned upon. Those who choose to do so will still see their fundamental needs met, but they would be entitled to a little less. What that might be may vary, but for one, you wouldn't be allowed to have children. To make it clear, you will still be allowed to marry if you find another with the same predisposition; you just won't be able to bring about children. This is not a punishment; it comes with the acknowledgment that children come with a lot of work and responsibility, and if one does not care to be of service to his brothers and sisters in society, how will they do so for a child, even one of their own? On the other hand, what would these parents pass on to their children, if anything? The nurturing of a society of light begins at home, with a lot of love, care, and attention. A dwelling that, with the support of society, nurtures understanding, respect, kindness, and wisdom.

Leadership

Leadership is a sensitive subject because it is, in essence, a position of influence, and those who seek it should probably not have it. In this society, no one should be able to manipulate and gain favor to crawl their way up into power. This point is key: if we transition to such a place, and this is a pretty big "if," we must ensure that the still very present mixed nature of this world doesn't ruin it all. So, every choice will be made based on merit, ability, and the right predisposition, and later on, I'll elaborate on how this might play out.

Leadership is about guiding and influencing outcomes, enabling people to work harmoniously together to achieve what they couldn't do alone. Those chosen to play such a role should be of strong character, wise, insightful, sensitive, supportive, open to different perspectives, and result-oriented. In such a society, I would not see this last one as a negative thing, but I would like to point out that outcomes are often enough out of our control, and what's important is to learn, adapt, and improve.

There is a new emerging approach to leadership that curiously fits into my idea of it. It is often described as "servant leadership." Some think of its name as demeaning, but I believe it conveys the right idea. The idea itself is simple: rather than being "the Boss," the one who orders, controls, and often demeans people, a more effective approach would be for leaders to be in service of the people they lead. The focus is on how leaders can make the lives of their team members easier—physically, cognitively, and emotionally, which will ultimately make them better in many ways. There is no thinking of oneself as superior due to position, skill, or knowledge. In fact, if something is gained in such a society, then it's immediately shared. If a new technology comes into play, and if it is for the benefit of all, then everyone should have it; the same goes if it comes to benefit a certain line of work.

Chapter Twelve
Language

I was only able to write my first book, *"The Life and Spiritual Journey of No One,"* because the English language had evolved to a certain point and certain concepts became more mainstream. Well, that combined with the fact that the consciousness of mankind was raised to a point where it was open enough to unlock certain things. This was made possible due to the actions of many good souls who have been paving the way to get here. We are all building upon each other's service, and rightly so. You may come to dissect this down to many levels, but what I do hope is that many will continue to work on this process.

OK, now more to the point. In 2024, there are 195 recognized countries in the world. This count includes 193 member countries of the United Nations and 2 observer states: the Holy See (Vatican City) and Palestine. The number of spoken languages in the world is a whole other matter. Disregarding slight fluctuations in numbers due to languages becoming extinct and new dialects being discovered or reclassified, the general consensus is that there are about seven thousand languages spoken worldwide. Yes, I said the staggering number of 7,000. However, we must not forget that some languages are more widely spoken than others.

Linguistics is the scientific study of language and its structure. It encompasses a broad range of topics and subfields, all aimed at understanding how languages work, how they are used, and how they evolve. Some of the key aspects of linguistics are phonology, morphology, syntax, semantics, pragmatics, sociolinguistics, psycholinguistics, etc. We do like to divide and classify, don't we? It would be painfully extensive and boring to speak about these to some measure. Instead, I will channel my exposition in a certain direction to make a point at the end.

Language is a reflection of how people think, feel, and act. Dialects and even slight variations like accents can reflect great deviations within the same people. One might say that these are a product of soil and weather. There are other factors at play, of course, but this apparently strange affirmation conveys an interesting truth, one that I will not explain at this point.

To understand different people, one has to learn their language to some detail, but this is not enough, and living in the same reality is a requirement to reach some level of understanding. This is a difficult and imperfect process that does not come close to those who are born and bred. More enlightened souls will come to understand a people through a slightly different process, but this is just not so for most.

Let me give you some personal examples that will further move us to the point I want to make: English, as you may know, is not my native language, but despite this fact, I chose to write my books in English. Well, in truth, this wasn't really a choice. I believe the spiritual experience that led me to speak and understand English overnight was the primary trigger for it. Ever since then, the thought process for certain subjects began to come to me in English. This fact, along with all other experiences in my life, ultimately drove me to write my first book in English many years later. On the other hand, I was meant to address certain subjects as they were given through the English language.

Many may come to ask why I did not translate my book into my mother tongue. The answer to this question will give a curious insight into the intricacies of language. I have nothing against translations, but whenever I tried to translate the content of my first book into my native tongue, I felt like something was lost. This turned out to be an actual fact, as it was conveyed with a number: 20% is lost. This truth will be further aggravated by relay translations, which is the process of translating a text from one language to another and then translating that translation into another language, and so on.

The barrier of language is much like the concepts of country and border. We see ourselves as different people and have a hard time understanding each other. Even if you come to know the language of someone else, that will only make you understand them at a very superficial level.

Unification

It seems to me that if we are to become one people, speaking the same language is part of the steps we have to take, and English just might play that part. Some of you might say that this is already at work, as English is already being taught as a second language in most countries in the world, which is true. However, what I'm actually suggesting is that English be taught as the first language everywhere in the world, until such time when it becomes the only one, at least for the most part.

Now, I'm not trying to brush the egos of those who are native speakers or to aggravate those who are not; it's just that English seems like the obvious choice. Some of you may feel that what I'm suggesting is robbing you of your heritage, and it is true that in certain instances in our human history, some have done so to undermine a people, which is "wrong." The point of all this is to bring us together, to make us one, not to tear us apart. This act will allow the merging of these different ways of thinking, feeling, and acting into one language, making the process of understanding each other easier. This may be a primitive first step, but a very necessary one.

Chapter Thirteen
Changes to Follow

There are some important changes that must follow the process initiated above. Most of these should be at play simultaneously, others will move in a slower pace in the process and a few should ideally be at work before this new society is at work. I speak in ideal timelines, but this might not come to be possible. Notwithstanding, all these changes will be fundamental in achieving the ultimate goal.

No Gambling

Any form of gambling has to be completely outlawed in this new society. The Mahabharata provides a story of an extreme nature that serves as a warning against gambling. It warns that even the most righteous of characters, which in this case is Yudhishthira, can fall victim to its temptations. Gambling can lead to ruin and chaos, not only for individuals but for entire families and societies. In this new world, gambling wouldn't even make sense, since there's no money or anything else to be gained, but I would still see men scheming to put something at work. I find this story quite relevant, and as such I'll share a more extensive outline of it:

In the grand halls of Hastinapura, a sense of anticipation hung heavy in the air. The Kauravas, led by the cunning Duryodhana, had extended an invitation to their cousins, the Pandavas, to participate in a game of dice. Yudhishthira, the eldest of the Pandavas and a man of unwavering righteousness, hesitated but felt compelled by his duty to accept. It was a decision driven by honor, though he knew all too well the dangers of gambling.

The Pandavas arrived at Hastinapura, their hearts filled with trepidation. The opulent hall was adorned with golden pillars and shimmering drapes, a fitting stage for what was to unfold. Duryodhana, seated with a sly smile, welcomed his cousins. At his side sat Shakuni, his maternal uncle and master of deceit, who would roll the dice on behalf of the Kauravas.

The game began innocently enough, with small wagers and friendly banter. But soon, Yudhishthira found himself on a losing streak. Each throw of the dice seemed to conspire against him, guided by Shakuni's skillful hand and perhaps the loaded dice he used. Desperation gnawed at Yudhishthira's resolve as he wagered his kingdom, his wealth, and his brothers, one by one.

With each loss, the tension in the hall grew palpable. The other Pandavas watched in helpless silence, bound by their loyalty to their eldest brother. Yudhishthira, unable to stop himself, continued to bet, hoping to reclaim what he had lost. The stakes climbed higher until finally, in a moment of reckless despair, he staked himself and his beloved wife, Draupadi.

The hall fell silent as Shakuni's dice sealed Yudhishthira's fate. The Kauravas erupted in jeering laughter, reveling in their triumph. Duryodhana, his eyes gleaming with malice, ordered Draupadi to be brought to the assembly hall. The noble queen was dragged in, her dignity affronted, her voice filled with righteous anger.

"How could my lord stake me when he had already lost himself?" she cried. Her plea for justice echoed through the hall, but it fell on deaf ears. Duryodhana, determined to humiliate the Pandavas further, ordered his brother Dushasana to disrobe Draupadi. The assembly watched in horror, their silence a testament to their powerlessness.

Draupadi, her honor at stake, invoked Lord Krishna with all her heart. In her moment of dire need, Krishna answered her prayers. As Dushasana pulled at her sari (traditional garment), it became endless, a divine miracle protecting her modesty. The Kauravas were confounded, their cruel intentions thwarted.

The elders of the assembly, Bhishma, Vidura, and even the blind King Dhritarashtra, were filled with shame and regret. Dhritarashtra, sensing the wrath of the gods and fearing the repercussions, offered Draupadi a boon. She asked for the freedom of her husbands, which was granted. When given a second boon, she requested the return of their lost wealth and kingdom. Dhritarashtra, eager to restore peace, complied.

But peace was fleeting. Duryodhana, fueled by his unrelenting hatred, challenged Yudhishthira to another game of dice. The stakes this time were even higher: the Pandavas' exile. Bound by his sense of honor and duty, Yudhishthira agreed. The outcome was inevitable—Shakuni's treachery prevailed, and the Pandavas were exiled to the forest for thirteen long years, with the stipulation that the final year be spent in incognito. If they were discovered, the exile would start anew.

As the Pandavas left Hastinapura, the clouds of destiny gathered. The game of dice had set in motion a chain of events that would lead to the great war of Kurukshetra, where the forces of Light and Darkness would clash in a battle for dharma. This story surprised me quite a bit, but it also made me acknowledge a larger truth, that under the right circumstances even the most virtuous can be led astray.

No Smoking

This one is kind of a no-brainer, since smoking is extremely hazardous for your health. I'm kind of speaking to the choir, but here is an outline of the consequences of smoking:

1. **<u>Respiratory Issues</u>:**

- **Chronic Obstructive Pulmonary Disease (COPD):** Smoking is a leading cause of COPD, including chronic bronchitis and emphysema, which cause long-term breathing problems.

- **Lung Cancer**: Smoking is the primary cause of lung cancer, responsible for approximately 85% of cases.

- **Respiratory Infections**: Smokers are more prone to infections such as pneumonia and tuberculosis.

2. <u>Cardiovascular Diseases</u>:

- **Heart Disease**: Smoking damages the heart and blood vessels, increasing the risk of heart attacks and strokes.

- **Peripheral Artery Disease (PAD)**: Smoking contributes to the narrowing and blockage of arteries in the limbs.

3. <u>Cancer</u>:

- **Various Types**: Besides lung cancer, smoking increases the risk of cancers of the mouth, throat, esophagus, bladder, pancreas, kidney, and cervix.

4. <u>Reproductive and Pregnancy Issues</u>:

- **Fertility Problems**: Smoking can reduce fertility in both men and women.

- **Complications During Pregnancy**: Smoking increases the risk of preterm birth, low birth weight, and stillbirth.

5. **<u>General Health Problems</u>**:

- **Weakened Immune System**: Smokers are more susceptible to infections.

- **Reduced Bone Health**: Smoking can lead to osteoporosis and fractures.

- **Gastrointestinal Issues**: It can cause peptic ulcers and Crohn's disease.

- **Skin Aging**: Smoking accelerates skin aging, leading to wrinkles and a dull complexion.

So, it should become obvious that smoking should be outlawed. Many may say, "I'm free to smoke if I want; it's my right." Yes, free will is a beautiful thing. However, we must acknowledge two things: Firstly, smoking is not just harmful to you, but also to those around you; and secondly, a society should not feed your ability to harm yourself.

On a lighter note, can you even remember what drove you to start smoking in the first place? I'm pretty sure it was for some silly reason, although it may not have seemed so at the time. Whatever the case may be, know that while quitting is overwhelmingly beneficial, it can also come with challenges to your health. So, just don't start.

Alcohol?

The risks and harms associated with drinking alcohol are well documented. The World Health Organization (WHO) states that there is no safe amount of alcohol consumption that does not affect health.

Alcohol's Inherent Dangers

Alcohol, is a toxic and dependence-producing substance, classified as a Group 1 carcinogen, alongside asbestos and tobacco. It causes at least seven types of cancer, including bowel and breast cancer. Any amount of alcohol, regardless of beverage type, poses a cancer risk.

Risk Increases with Consumption

Even light to moderate drinking significantly increases cancer risk. In the WHO European Region, half of all alcohol-attributable cancers are caused by low and moderate levels of consumption. The risk starts from the first drop, and the more you drink, the greater the harm.

No Safe Threshold

No scientific evidence supports a "safe" level of alcohol consumption. While some studies suggest potential benefits for cardiovascular health, these do not outweigh the cancer risks. "The risk to health starts from the first drop," says Dr. Carina Ferreira-Borges of WHO Europe.

Reflections/Suggestions

This is a somewhat tricky subject. If the mixed nature of the world remains prevalent at the start of this society, it will be difficult to completely ban alcohol consumption, no matter how much we strive to increase public awareness. The issue is that even if we exclude those with serious problems, there are still many who view alcohol consumption as a social activity, a form of social gratification. They often believe that others won't accept them unless they have a drink in hand or go along with the group. This new society will not encourage this predisposition, but even so, I believe it will be difficult to eliminate. Therefore, my advice would be to implement some controls: These beverages should only be available in certain social establishments, served within specific limits along with juices, milkshakes, and, yes, water. They should be served only on specific days and at predetermined hours. Those who refuse to do any form of work will, of course, be banned from consuming alcohol.

It is difficult for me to plan for an uncertain circumstance, but reducing alcohol consumption is crucial, as less alcohol means lower health risks and more focused minds. Humanity will eventually overcome the desire for such things; we just have to persist in guiding it properly.

No TV

Television has been around for nearly a century. It saw small developments over the decades until the arrival of color television and satellite TV between the 1960s and 1980s. However, it was the 1990s that brought about the greatest advancements, shaping television into what it is today.

Television has played its role in shaping modern entertainment, culture, and communication, but it has no place in this new society. I don't mean to sound self-righteous: I do watch television, just not in a conventional form. My personal balance requires me to see things that lift my heart and spirit, and since I'm unable to find them in real life, I seek them in movies and shows. However, these are few in number and far between. Books serve the same purpose, but they lack the fast-forward option that I'm so keen on using.

There are indeed times when something good is conveyed through this platform. However, television has mostly become a distraction, and an instrument that feeds our fears and desires. As such, it has no place in the development of a utopian society, and this goes for TV, cinema, and theater alike.

Many of you will think: *"Oh my Lord, what will we do?"*, which is a curious worry. Firstly, we have to acknowledge that television and its variants are more of a negative influence than anything else. Secondly, we are striving to create a society that encourages interaction with your brothers and sisters, nurturing a community of harmony and care. Thirdly, other technologies will emerge that will grant you positive opportunities, just as long as you don't become too attached to them. Lastly, this state of affairs will ultimately encourage those who do nothing to seek otherwise.

No Social Media

As mankind evolved, the means of connecting with one another advanced significantly. Alongside the transportation milestones of boats, trains, cars, and airplanes, communication technology also saw remarkable advancements. Telephones bridged the gap of instant voice communication, making it possible to speak with someone miles away in real-time. Radio brought news and entertainment to the masses, uniting people with a shared experience. Television added a visual dimension to this shared experience, creating a powerful medium for information and culture dissemination.

In the digital age, the internet emerged as a transformative force, taking interconnectedness to an entirely new level, and of course, social media is very much a part of that. However, it's not all sunshine and roses, as social media has brought about some troublesome developments in society.

Social media has come to expose sensitive information, making users vulnerable to identity theft and cyber exploitation. Additionally, the anonymity of social media platforms has fueled cyberbullying and harassment, causing severe emotional distress, especially among younger users. Misinformation spreads rapidly on these platforms, blurring the lines between truth and falsehood, and influencing public opinion in harmful ways. Furthermore, social media has become a hotspot for scams and blackmail, preying on the unsuspecting and eroding trust and security online.

It becomes evident that, much like television, social media has become little more than a negative instrument. It would be acceptable if social media were just a neutral distraction, for we all, from time to time, need some distraction from this troublesome life. However, most of its content is garbage, and it will definitely turn your brain into mush. We live in an age of unprecedented interconnectedness, but we are more disconnected than ever before. As such, it would be very counter-productive to allow such a thing to exist in the process of developing a better society.

No Pets

I know that this step will aggrieve those who love their pets, but hear me out. I'm not questioning that some of you do love and properly care for your pets; that is not the point of this exposition. However, mankind has created quite a big problem with no immediate solution. We strive to address it by creating animal shelters and protective associations, but they ultimately solve nothing. Some countries create protective laws that do improve the current circumstances, but the underlying problem remains.

What is the underlying problem? Us. We take natural-born predators from their natural habitats, breed them to our wants, and imprison them in our homes and cities. We effectively take away the ability of these carnivores to feed themselves, which in turn leads us to kill in order to feed them. There are all kinds of wrong surrounding this, and one builds upon the other.

Having a pet is not a need; it is a want. You may feel the need to save or take in a stray, and it may be right to do so in this imperfect world, but realize that you are still feeding the problem. The wants that drive us can vary greatly: you may want a dog to protect you, a "true" friend, or one who loves you unconditionally. I could deconstruct all of these, which will not be to your pleasure. However, the one who should really answer this question is you.

In a society that strives to breed love and harmony between brethren, why would you want to have a pet?

No Competitions

Here I'm going to speak about sports competitions, but this should apply to all aspects of life. There should be no more sports competitions, professional or otherwise. I know that this will upset many, for they feel that this is the only thing they have to look forward to in life. I have to admit that there is beauty in something that is done with heart and spirit, but the same could be said about everything else, not just in sports. The stories of struggle, courage, difficulty, and pain, of overcoming against all odds, do move and inspire us, but these are exceptions, very few in number.

Don't get me wrong, exercise and some sports should still be very much a part of our lives, but we should nurture a different predisposition toward them, and this may come to express itself in many ways. There is very little to be gained through competition, and we have to admit that it doesn't bring out the best in people, quite the opposite. This new society should be very attentive, for even without competitions, negative behavior will still have a tendency to spring out, and when that happens it should be immediately reproached and corrected by all who see it, but never in a violent way.

Foster Cooperation, Not Competition

I will strive to explain this by using the Universal process as an example. Mankind lives in the plane of the Self-aware, and in order to move into the plane of Love and Understanding (Fourth Plane), one has to make his own fundamental choice which will lead him to move through the ways of the positive (Light) or the negative (Darkness). Those who choose to follow the path of Light will see themselves in the Fourth Plane of existence where the focus is on Love and Understanding one another. This plane of existence can be showered with some wisdom, of course, but the focus should always be Love and Understanding. The reason behind this is simple: to create a people of one heart and mind. Such a social-memory-complex withholds nothing, manipulates nothing, and cares for everything. This state of being and reflective predisposition ushers entry into the Cycle of Wisdom, that in the spirit of **cooperation**, comes to see unprecedented spiritual and material growth. **Competition** moves in the way of self-interest, which will breed a different environment and results.

Some Thoughts

This book is meant to engage you in your own process of reflection without guiding you too forcefully. That level of personal involvement is necessary to inspire meaningful change. I have no control over what you choose to see or not see—at best, I can take you to the edge of your own thinking. Where you go from there is up to each and every one of us.

With that said, I understand that some of the ideas presented in this chapter may create emotional resistance. Often, this reflects our attachment to a particular time, place, or way of living.

These attachments are deeply personal. Many cherish their pets; others enjoy smoking, drinking, gambling, or turning to television and social media. I will not dwell on each of these, but I will use pets as an example. What defines a "good" pet varies greatly, and many of these animals still play a role in our lives—as we do in theirs—for better or worse. That reality will not change overnight.

What I ask of you is this: where do you see humanity evolving? In a truly harmonious society, do you envision everyone having a pet? Which ones—and at what cost? Perhaps such things would remain, but in a different form, shaped by a deeper understanding and responsibility.

Change, in many of these areas, will be gradual and shaped by circumstance. Even if you view human progress in purely physical or linear terms, do not become fixed in that view. Strive to keep an open mind—and, more importantly, an open heart.

Chapter Fourteen
Healthcare

Healthcare is an essential pillar of society, encompassing a broad range of services aimed at promoting, maintaining, and restoring health. At its core, healthcare is about people - from the dedicated professionals who deliver care to the patients who rely on their expertise. There are public and private healthcare systems, but I will not compare or speak in detail about them here. Instead, I aim to address the cost of healthcare, especially for those without insurance. The private sector is the proper target for this subject, and I'll use the U.S. as the center of this exposition.

Below is a linear exposition of average American healthcare prices for common procedures and services. While there may be some variation depending on the healthcare facility providing the services, this will give you a good overview of the costs you may incur when visiting a doctor or hospital without insurance. These are also the prices a visitor to the U.S. may face if they do not have a travel insurance plan or international health insurance plan.

Healthcare Costs in the USA

Emergency Room Visit

- **Ambulance**: $400+
- **Tests**: $100 to $500
- **Overnight stay**: $5,000
- **Medications**: Varies
- **Total**: $6,000+

Cancer Treatment (Without Insurance)

- **Bone marrow transplant**: $638,000 to $900,000+
- **Brain cancer**: $50,000 to $700,000+
- **Breast cancer**: $48,500 to $300,000+
- **Pancreatic cancer**: $31,000 to $200,000+
- **Melanoma**: $1,700 to $152,000+

Common Lab Tests (Without Insurance)

- **MRI scan**: $500 to $7,850+
- **Blood test**: $40 to $3,000+
- **Cholesterol test (walk-in clinic)**: $50 to $130+
- **Cholesterol test (at-home kit)**: $40 to $75+
- **X-ray**: $200 to $3,000+

Prescription Drugs

- **Insulin (for diabetes)**: $530 to $1,100+
- **Allergy shots (per year)**: $600 to $2,000+
- **Cholesterol medication**: $30 to $130
- **Asthma inhalers**: $60 to $70+

Family Planning (Without Insurance)

- **Doctor's visit (pre-natal care)**: $100 to $2,000+

- **Labor and delivery**: $2,700 to $40,100+
- **Cesarean section**: $10,600 to $50,500+
- **Postpartum check-up**: $100 to $3,100+
- **Birth complications**: $3,000+ per day
- **NICU stay (20 days average)**: $60,000+

Surgery (Without Insurance)

- **Coronary artery bypass**: $21,500 to $254,000+
- **Appendectomy**: $1,800 to $82,000+
- **Gallbladder removal**: $8,000 to $54,000+
- **Hysterectomy**: $8,700 to $40,000+
- **Cataract surgery**: $330 to $12,000+
- **Tonsillectomy**: $790 to $12,000+

Broken Bones or Sprains

- **Hip fracture**: $16,000 to $53,000+
- **Sprained/broken ankle (non-surgical)**: $300+
- **Sprained/broken ankle (surgical)**: $17,000 to $20,000+
- **Sprained/broken wrist (non-surgical)**: $500+
- **Sprained/broken wrist (surgical)**: $7,000 to $10,000+
- **Physical therapy**: $120 to $350 per session

A visit to the doctor's office is relatively affordable. An initial consultation with a doctor will cost around $100 to $200. However, if you are ill, additional costs will become expensive quickly. Visits to specialists are typically more expensive depending on their specialty and the nature of your visit. On average, specialists will charge $250 or more for a consultation. I will not address the high cost of all this, just keep it in mind as we continue with the flow of this book.

The Cost of Medical Care in America with Insurance

Navigating healthcare costs in the U.S. can be daunting, but having health insurance can significantly mitigate these expenses. For those living abroad or visiting, purchasing an international health insurance plan is a prudent choice. While it requires paying a regular premium, it safeguards you against potentially exorbitant medical bills.

A good insurance plan typically covers most of your healthcare costs, except for a deductible and co-pay. Plans with higher deductibles and co-pays usually have lower premiums, and vice versa. Some plans cover all expenses without limits, but others have a "medical maximum," capping the amount the insurance will pay. Choosing a plan with a lower medical maximum can reduce your premiums but increases your financial risk if your medical costs exceed this limit.

The cost of health insurance in the U.S. varies widely. Comprehensive international health insurance plans, which provide extensive coverage, can cost around $500 per month on average. Though this might seem steep, it is a reasonable price compared to potentially facing an incredibly high medical bill.

Healthcare Costs in The USA vs Other Private Healthcare Systems

Healthcare costs in the United States are significantly higher than in other countries with predominantly private healthcare systems. Here's a comparison of costs for common medical procedures in the U.S. versus other nations with similar private healthcare models, such as Switzerland, Singapore, and South Korea.

Emergency Room Visits

In the U.S., an emergency room visit can easily cost $1,200 or more, with additional charges for tests and overnight stays potentially bringing the total to over $6,000. In contrast, an emergency room visit in Switzerland typically costs around $700, including basic tests and treatments. In Singapore, the cost is even lower, generally ranging from $75 to $200, thanks to efficient healthcare practices and cost-control measures within their private system.

Childbirth

Childbirth in the U.S. can be overwhelming financially. A standard delivery typically costs between $10,000 and $15,000, while a cesarean section can range from $20,000 to $50,000. In Switzerland, the cost of childbirth, including a cesarean section, is about $7,500 to $10,000. In South Korea, where advanced medical facilities are prevalent, childbirth costs are approximately $1,500 to $3,000, depending on the complexity of the delivery and the chosen hospital.

Imaging and Diagnostic Tests

In the U.S., an MRI scan can cost anywhere from $500 to $3,000, depending on the facility and region. In South Korea, the same MRI scan might cost between $300 and $500. In Switzerland, the cost ranges from $400 to $800, benefiting from advanced medical technology and effective cost management in their private healthcare system.

Prescription Medications

The cost of prescription medications is another area where the U.S. stands out. A monthly supply of insulin for diabetes can cost between $300 and $1,000 in the U.S. However, in Switzerland, the cost is typically around $50 to $150 per month due to regulated pricing and efficient distribution. In Singapore, the price is about $100 to $200 per month, reflecting a balance between quality and affordability within their private sector.

Reflections

Well, I'll tell you this: whether on the upper or lower end of these examples, most of the citizens in my country would be dead, for there is no way most of them could afford any of this. Many will say that the high prices of healthcare in the United States can be attributed to the complexity of the healthcare system, the influence of various interest groups, and specific economic and policy conditions. This is a very politically correct way of saying much and explaining little, but I do agree that there are many interests at play.

I'm not even going to try and address what a fair price is, because even disregarding important factors, this will vary as much as the minds in question. However, I will say this: Your brothers' and sisters' health is not a business, but everyone's business. Healthcare is a fundamental need, and all should have access to it. Mankind is still in a very primitive stage in regards to medical development. I believe that in time, more cost-effective technologies will come into play. This will include scanning technology, sound/frequency treatments, stem cells, nanobiotechnology, light treatments, and more.

On the other hand, we should all realize that good health starts by taking care of ourselves. I have come to realize that our wellbeing lies in achieving a balance between the spiritual and material, and this will imply a number of different things. However, I do realize that some of you may not be in a place that cares for the spiritual aspects of your life, but your predisposition towards your physical self should be the same whether you are in a spiritual process or not. Overall wellbeing depends on how you relax, how you sleep, proper exercise, hydration, what you eat, when you eat and how much. Incorporate activities you love, whether it's dancing, hiking, or playing a sport, to make staying active enjoyable. Practice mindfulness, spend time with loved ones, and take breaks when needed. Remember, taking care of yourself isn't a luxury; it's a necessity, and a good society should properly accommodate for it.

Chapter Fifteen
Diets – Vegetarianism

Food plays a crucial role in achieving healthy, balanced living. I touched on this in my first book, but it essentially comes down to what you eat, when you eat, and how much you eat. I refrained from giving strict advice even within the vegetarian diet, because what works best depends on the individual and their particular circumstances. Instead, I provided tools and guidelines to help each person develop their own diet.

I am currently a vegetarian, but there are many other diets, and most include eating fish and meat. I refrain from passing any linear judgment on them, mostly because we are born into them, much like I was. It's just that we don't give it a second thought. Things are not always simple, as you will come to see from this exposition. Looking at different approaches from a religious perspective, such as Hindu, Buddhist, Jewish, and Islamic practices, will help somewhat.

HINDU DIET

General Principles:

- **Ahimsa (Non-violence):** Strong emphasis on non-violence, which extends to animals.

- **Purity:** Food and drink should promote spiritual and physical purity.

Common Practices:

- **Vegetarianism:** Avoiding meat and eggs is common among devout Hindus. Traditionally, eggs were banned in Hinduism because it was impossible to ensure they weren't fertilized, which could mean taking animal life. Today, commercially sold eggs are unfertilized, so this issue no longer exists.

- **Lacto-vegetarianism:** Dairy products are consumed.

- **Avoidance of Certain Foods:** Beef is strictly avoided because the cow is considered sacred.

- **Fasting:** Regular fasting days and periods such as Ekadashi, Navratri, and during festivals.

Rituals:

- **Prasadam:** Food offered to deities and then consumed by devotees.

- **Sattvic Diet:** Emphasizes foods that promote clarity and tranquility, avoiding foods considered rajasic (stimulating) or tamasic (dulling).

BUDDHIST DIET

General Principles:

- **Ahimsa (Non-violence):** Similar to Hinduism, emphasis on non-harming.

- **Mindful Eating:** Focus on mindful consumption and awareness of the impact of food choices.

Common Practices:

- **Vegetarianism:** Encouraged, especially among monks and devout practitioners.

- **Varies by Sect and Region:** Some sects and cultures permit meat if the animal was not killed specifically for the consumer.

- **Avoiding Certain Foods:** Garlic, onions, and strong spices may be avoided in some traditions due to their stimulating effects.

Rituals:

- **Dana:** Offering food to monks and the poor.

- **Fasting:** Practiced on certain days and during specific periods.

<u>JEWISH DIET</u>

General Principles:

- **Kashrut (Dietary Laws):** Set of Jewish dietary laws derived from the Torah.

Common Practices:

- **Kosher:** Food that complies with kashrut, including specific rules about how animals are slaughtered and which foods can be eaten together.

- **Prohibited Foods:** Pork, shellfish, and certain other animals.

- **Separation of Meat and Dairy:** Not consuming meat and dairy products together.

- **Blessings:** Reciting blessings before and after eating.

Rituals:

- **Passover:** Special dietary restrictions, including avoiding leavened bread.

- **Sabbath Meals:** Specific foods and traditions for Sabbath meals.

ISLAMIC DIET

General Principles:

- **Halal (Permissible):** Foods and drinks that are allowed under Islamic law.

- **Haram (Forbidden):** Foods and drinks that are prohibited.

Common Practices:

- **Halal Meat:** Meat must be slaughtered in the name of Allah and in a specific manner.

- **Prohibited Foods:** Pork and its by-products, alcohol, and any intoxicants.

- **Fasting:** During Ramadan, Muslims fast from dawn until sunset.

Rituals:

- **Ramadan:** Month-long fasting period with specific meals for pre-dawn (Suhoor) and post-sunset (Iftar).

- **Eid al-Adha:** Ritual animal sacrifice and sharing of meat.

- **Dua:** Reciting prayers before and after meals.

I've provided a general outline of the dietary practices in different religions. I haven't discussed Christianity because there is no general direction to it. Jesus Christ was Jewish, so for the most part, he followed Jewish guidelines, but there is no recorded evidence that he ate meat. The Catholic Church probably carried some ill feelings toward the Jews due to Jesus' crucifixion, or maybe they just wanted to distance themselves from Jewish practice. Given that this is mostly conjecture, I will no longer speak of it.

Firstly, we must acknowledge that the dietary practices in Hinduism, Buddhism, Judaism, and Islam were deeply influenced by the context of food scarcity, diversity, and availability in their respective environments. Hinduism and Buddhism originated in the Indian subcontinent, a region known for its diverse and rich environment, including fertile land and abundant water sources. This region supported a wide variety of crops, spices, fruits, vegetables, and grains, enabling a predominantly vegetarian diet that is tasty and balanced. Judaism and Islam emerged in the

Middle East, characterized by arid and semi-arid climates with limited agricultural diversity and water resources. Livestock played a crucial role due to the suitability of animals like sheep, goats, and camels for these environments. Kashrut and halal laws developed in response to the practicalities and ethical considerations of raising and consuming animals in a resource-scarce environment, which brings about a curious point I want to make.

Kashrut (Jewish dietary laws) and halal (Islamic dietary laws) have several similarities, particularly in their methods of making food suitable for consumption. One of them is that blood must be completely drained from the slaughtered animal because consuming blood is forbidden. I find this to be a very curious and important detail. Both these religions have seen great souls come into the Earth to help and guide; they recognized the circumstance of certain people and saw that abiding by vegetarian guidelines would be extremely difficult, if not impossible. As such, they accommodated for the possibility, but not without conveying a universal distaste for blood. This process holds significant importance for both Jewish and Islamic religions, yet it still involves the drawing of blood. Although eating meat doesn't inherently make you violent, it does feed an already very violent human nature.

On a second note, we must recognize that there is a Higher Mind at work. For someone with a food safety background, it is curious to see the ban on pork and shellfish in ancient cultures and religions. In the food industry, these are considered high-risk foods—the first being prolific with parasites, and the second abundant with viruses, bacteria, and high levels of cadmium and arsenic. It would be impossible for such underdeveloped cultures to know such things, much less protect themselves from them.

Vegetarianism: A Worldwide Diet

There are many places in the world that struggle with poverty and limited resources, making it hard to worry about a proper diet. However, in many places in the developed world, food scarcity, diversity, and availability are no longer issues, and a balanced vegetarian diet is possible. Is it not?

Again, this is not that simple. Despite best efforts, many still struggle with it. Why is that? The answer is simple, yet complex. We struggle with a vegetarian diet because we are not born into it, not in the sense that we don't know how to make it balanced or tasty—which is true—but in a very biological way.

Our gut flora, the complex community of microorganisms living in our digestive tracts, is largely inherited from our parents. This microbial inheritance can significantly influence our ability to adapt to different diets. If our ancestors were not primarily vegetarians, our gut flora might not easily adapt to a vegetarian diet. This is because the microbes in our gut play a crucial role in digesting and extracting nutrients from the food we eat. (**See Appendix Three**)

For generations, our ancestors' diets shaped their gut microbiomes to efficiently process the foods they commonly consumed. Those whose diets included meat and animal products would have developed a gut flora adept at breaking down these foods. Conversely, vegetarians would have cultivated a different microbial profile, better suited to processing plant-based foods.

Therefore, when someone with a lineage of omnivores adopts a vegetarian diet, their gut flora might struggle to fully adapt. This can lead to challenges in extracting all necessary nutrients from plant-based foods. Over time, the gut flora can adjust to new dietary habits, but this can be challenging. The approach I give in my first book will help greatly in this process, but it is still not easy. In India, I was quite surprised to see how balanced and tasty a vegetarian diet could actually be, but I just couldn't reproduce it at home. Yes, it is possible to create a balanced diet in your own country, but this will require knowledge, aptitude, and some experience. However, I feel we will always fall short on variety and taste. We should learn from the best examples if our global society is to become vegetarian; in time, we would easily transition into it. In my estimate, this could take one or two generations.

Chapter Sixteen
Food Safety

Food safety encompasses the practices and conditions necessary to ensure that food is safe to consume and free from contaminants that could cause harm to human health. It is a multifaceted discipline, integrating science, regulations, and consumer awareness to prevent foodborne illnesses and protect public health. The journey of food from farm to table involves numerous steps where potential hazards must be managed, including production, processing, storage, distribution, and preparation.

The Path to Safe Food: From Farm to Fork

Imagine the path of a single apple. It begins its journey in an orchard, where it is nurtured by careful agricultural practices that minimize the use of harmful pesticides and ensure the soil is free from contaminants. Farmers follow stringent guidelines to maintain hygiene and monitor the health of their crops, which is the first critical step in food safety.

Once harvested, the apple is transported to a processing facility. Here, it undergoes rigorous cleaning and inspection processes to remove any dirt, debris, or microorganisms. This step is crucial, as contamination can easily spread during processing if proper hygiene standards are not upheld. Modern food safety protocols often include the use of advanced technology like ultraviolet light or ozone treatments to ensure that the food is as safe as possible before it reaches the consumer.

During transportation to markets and stores, the apple must be kept at the right temperature to prevent spoilage. Cold chain management, which maintains the appropriate temperature throughout the supply chain, plays a vital role in food safety. Any break in this chain can lead to the growth of harmful bacteria, making the food unsafe to eat.

Once in the hands of consumers, the responsibility of food safety shifts to individuals. Proper handling, storage, and preparation of food at home are critical. Washing hands before handling food, cooking at the right temperatures, and storing food properly to avoid cross-contamination are all essential practices, and these should be a part of everyone's education.

I worked in this field for some time, and I've seen some crazy stuff, but never have I heard of such extremes as in the US—the best and the worst. Don't get me wrong, this is a worldwide problem, and people, if left unchecked, will do the craziest things for a little profit. Some of the best practices and educational material I've seen come from the US, but then comes the other part that I just can't understand.

New Health Issue: Fruits and Vegetables in the United States

In the United States, fruits and vegetables, once considered some of the safest foods, are now emerging as significant health concerns. This shift has been alarming, as these foods are integral to a healthy diet, providing essential nutrients, vitamins, and minerals. However, recent outbreaks of foodborne illnesses linked to produce have raised questions about the effectiveness of current food safety practices and regulatory measures.

The Unexpected Risks of Fruits and Vegetables

Traditionally, the focus of food safety efforts has been on potentially hazardous foods like meat, dairy, and seafood, which are more prone to bacterial contamination and spoilage. Fruits and vegetables were seen as relatively safe, often requiring only basic washing before consumption. However, in recent years, there have been numerous high-profile outbreaks of illnesses linked to produce. Contaminations involving E. coli, Salmonella, and Listeria have been traced back to leafy greens, melons, and other fresh produce, causing serious illnesses and even fatalities.

These new emerging risks in fruits and vegetables are not the problem in themselves. They are bound to occur, especially if there's a change in circumstance. The real problem is not addressing these new issues properly. The U.S. Food and Drug

Administration (FDA) and the Centers for Disease Control and Prevention (CDC) are the primary agencies responsible for overseeing food safety, but they appear to be struggling to effectively address the problem. If there is indeed an incapability of the current agencies to address these problems, which I find strange, then a new one with appropriate power should come into play.

Class of Citizens

To close, I would like to give a very pertinent example that goes with the flow of what I speak. The United States armed forces don't seem to be struggling with this issue, or any other related to food safety. Ask yourselves: do they have the same supplier as the general public? Do they have the same checks and controls? I believe the answer is obvious. The US armed forces have to be battle-ready in an instant, so it is unthinkable to have their forces decommissioned due to such a basic need as food. The government wants their soldiers to be ripe for combat, not rotten; the battle would be lost before it even started. So, as you see, we have two different classes of citizens right here. Food safety is a fundamental need for all human beings, and I do mean all.

It really doesn't matter if a certain food looks tasty or if it's nutritious if it ends up killing you or making you sick. Paying for it doesn't make a difference, but it does aggravate things. You know, I studied and taught these things for years, but I did take them a little lightly until I experienced them myself. Here we are essentially talking about poison, and it can kill you in a very painful way or leave you scarred for life. So, as you can now understand, food safety is a basic prerequisite for everything that follows.

Chapter Seventeen
Food Quality

The quality of what we eat is, and always has been, fundamental to our health. Yet, we find ourselves entrenched in a culture of junk food, with the United States often seen as the epitome of this trend. The convenience, affordability, and pervasive marketing of processed foods have shaped dietary habits, creating a landscape where fast-food chains and sugary snacks dominate.

The rise of junk food can be traced back to the mid-20th century, a time when food technology innovations promised convenience and longer shelf life. These developments aligned perfectly with the fast-paced lifestyle that was becoming the norm. The post-war era saw a boom in consumerism, and the food industry responded with an array of processed options that were cheap, tasty, and easy to prepare. Over time, these foods have become staples in many households, displacing traditional, nutrient-rich meals.

Junk food's appeal lies in its design; it's engineered to be hyper-palatable, with precise combinations of sugar, salt, and fat that trigger pleasure centers in the brain. This creates a cycle of craving and consumption that's hard to break. Advertising, particularly aimed at children, reinforces this cycle, embedding the preference for junk food early in life. Brightly colored packaging, catchy jingles, and the promise of instant gratification make resisting these foods a daunting challenge.

However, the consequences of this dietary shift are stark. The prevalence of junk food is closely linked to rising rates of obesity, diabetes, heart disease, and other chronic health conditions. These foods are typically high in calories but low in essential nutrients, leading to a phenomenon known as "hidden hunger" where individuals consume enough calories but lack vital nutrients. This nutritional imbalance affects physical health, cognitive function, and overall well-being.

The social implications are equally troubling. Healthcare systems are burdened with the treatment of diet-related illnesses, leading to increased medical costs and reduced quality of life for millions. I'm never really surprised by our ability to harm ourselves, but it should really come into question why our society not only feeds but promotes it.

The importance of quality food cannot be overstated. Whole foods, rich in nutrients, support optimal health and prevent disease. Diets abundant in fruits, vegetables, whole grains, lean proteins, and healthy fats provide the body with essential vitamins, minerals, and antioxidants. These nutrients are crucial for maintaining a robust immune system, promoting mental clarity, and ensuring energy levels remain stable throughout the day.

Quality food also fosters a deeper connection to what we eat and where it comes from. We are what we eat, that is true, but the quality of what we eat is also bound by our actions, whether they involve whole foods or not. The whole point of eating quality foods, like fruits and vegetables, is to receive their rich nutritional content. However, due to various agricultural practices, the soils have become greatly depleted, and such foods no longer fulfill that promise.

Soil and Farming

I haven't dwelled on this subject since my college days. At the time, the fad was organic farming, but it has always been hard for me to be a fan of something that very few can afford. But this is just one point.

Organic Farming

Organic farming is a holistic approach to agriculture that prioritizes the health of the environment, animals, and people. It eschews synthetic pesticides and fertilizers, genetically modified organisms (GMOs), and practices that can harm the ecosystem, in favor of natural processes that sustain soil fertility, conserve water, and promote biodiversity.

However, the effectiveness of organic farming in achieving its goals is greatly questioned. Some critics argue that organic farming has not fully delivered on its promises, pointing to continued soil depletion and concerns over the nutritional content of organic produce.

One of the challenges organic farming faces is maintaining soil health in the long term. While organic practices like composting, crop rotations, and green manure contribute to soil fertility, they may not always fully counteract the depletion caused by continuous cropping and other agricultural demands. In some cases, organic farms have struggled with lower yields compared to conventional farms, which can lead to over-cultivation and soil degradation.

Nutritional content is another area where organic farming has faced scrutiny. Some studies suggest that the nutrient levels in organic produce can vary widely depending on factors such as soil quality, crop variety, and farming practices. While organic foods often have higher levels of certain nutrients and lower levels of pesticide residues, the overall nutritional difference compared to conventional produce is sometimes less pronounced than expected.

Organic farming prides itself on relying less on synthetic chemicals, which can have harmful effects on the environment and human health. However, humankind has brought about so much corruption that it will be difficult to face disease and pests without resorting more to man-made pesticides. More research should be conducted on these to ensure that whatever is used does not negatively affect the environment, human health, and the gene pool of the plants in question.

It's also good to be aware that this form of farming yields fruits and vegetables of smaller proportion and greater imperfection, which would be acceptable if they brought about greater nutritional content, but they do not. The core problem still remains: the soil. We take so much and give nothing back, or not nearly enough. This problem is not particular to any one country; it's a worldwide issue. Fortunately, nothing is really lost, just transformed and in this case misplaced, and what follows next may give an adequate answer.

Regenerative Agriculture

Regenerative agriculture is an innovative farming approach that goes beyond traditional sustainable practices, aiming to restore and enhance the health of ecosystems. At its core, regenerative agriculture seeks to replenish and rejuvenate soil, increase biodiversity, and improve water cycles, all while producing nutritious food. Unlike conventional farming, which often depletes resources, regenerative agriculture works harmoniously with nature, creating a self-sustaining system. Well, at least more effectively than organic farming.

The principles of regenerative agriculture include minimizing soil disturbance through reduced or no-till farming, using cover crops to protect and enrich soil, and integrating livestock to mimic natural grazing patterns. These methods help build soil organic matter, improving soil structure and fertility. Healthier soil retains more water and nutrients, reducing the need for chemical fertilizers and irrigation, and making crops more resilient to droughts and floods.

Biodiversity is another cornerstone of regenerative agriculture. By planting a diverse array of crops and integrating agroforestry practices, farmers can create habitats for beneficial insects and wildlife. This diversity not only supports pest management but also enhances ecosystem stability. Polycultures and crop rotations break pest and disease cycles, reducing the need for synthetic pesticides.

Livestock integration is a unique aspect of regenerative farming. Managed grazing can help regenerate grasslands, as the natural behaviors of animals stimulate plant growth and nutrient cycling. This symbiotic relationship between plants and animals mimics natural ecosystems, leading to healthier soils and pastures.

Regenerative agriculture also emphasizes the importance of community and farmer well-being. By fostering local food systems and supporting farmers with fair wages and training, this approach contributes to social sustainability. It encourages a deep connection between people and the land, promoting stewardship and long-term thinking.

The importance of regenerative agriculture cannot be overstated. As the global population continues to grow and climate change threatens food security, regenerative practices offer a viable path forward. They not only provide immediate benefits, such as increased crop yields and farm profitability, but also long-term advantages like carbon sequestration and ecosystem restoration. By healing the land and creating resilient agricultural systems, regenerative agriculture paves the way for a more sustainable and equitable future for all.

Chapter Eighteen

Exercise

Here, I could give another linear textbook exposition about exercise, how it's good for this and that, but the truth is that most of you who are reading this are either already exercising or are in a place where you really don't care for it. As such, I will not bore you with things you already know. Instead, I'll share some insights that will benefit those who are already engaged in physical activities and maybe inspire those who aren't.

I have always had a sense of responsibility towards the body I was given. I felt the need to take care of it and make it better if I could. As such, I strived to do so to the best of my ability at any given time, and of course, that aptitude to care for myself grew over time. During my spiritual journey, I did stop for quite some time. I was unsure of the best course of action, and receiving advice from those who do not practice what they preach didn't help. However, due to my ordeals, stopping at the time was the best course of action, just not for such a long time.

We are physical beings, and our musculoskeletal system is a big part of that. Consequently, one must do some physical work to keep it in proper working order. As they say: if you don't use it, you lose it. It's difficult for me to explain to what heights of well-being our bodies can be taken, but I would say almost superhuman.

At this point, everything seems to be functioning at its peak, your mind is focused, your body is strong and highly responsive, and you feel powerful, like you could do anything. I remember thinking many years later that if this state were balanced with the spiritual side of our existence, it would be something extraordinary to feel and behold. However, could've, should've, would've are pointless thoughts and don't really help anyone. Much of this is probably inconceivable for most, and we tend to think of ourselves as healthy due to the absence of external symptoms of disease, but this is not true and not the proper frame of mind.

Food and Exercise

I have heard many say: I eat healthy and walk a lot, and I believe this is enough to keep me healthy. Firstly, I do not consider walking a form of exercise; it's just something you should already be doing in your day-to-day life. Secondly, healthy and balanced eating is not enough to keep you healthy. Food and exercise are deeply interconnected. I like to say that how you eat determines success, and how you train determines shape and performance. Realize also that proper exercise keeps the juices flowing to all the right places. In other words, proper exercise will ensure that the nutrients you eat will flow to where they are needed, and this will happen on a day-to-day basis, not just when you exercise. On the other hand, muscles are the greatest metabolic organ in our bodies, and for that and many other reasons, it is in our best interest to maintain them.

What Form of Exercise

This is a complicated subject because the appropriate answer will depend greatly on the individual in question. In my years of experience, I've come to realize that if a client is unhappy with a certain diet, their subconscious mind will take action, and nothing will work no matter how good or healthy the diet is. The same thing can be said about exercise. It is extremely important to find something you like, not just for effectiveness, but to keep going over time. A proper society should accommodate possibilities and never impose a certain form of exercise on its people, no matter how good it is.

With that said, keep in mind that our bodies need a certain level of strength training to maintain muscle structure, and more so to gain it. You can combine different activities, mixing what is effective with what you enjoy. You may like dancing, cycling, hatha yoga, or whatever, but that does not exclude the need for other forms of physical conditioning.

I do realize that no matter what I say, or how easy I make it, many will still not care for it. The same thing can be said about healthy eating or meditation. Most of us are just not in that place. Taking care of yourself through wholesome living is not a guarantee of not getting sick, for this world is prolific in agents of decay. However, your actions will either make your body a breeding ground for them or a vessel that prevents and controls them. I hope that most of these expositions will make you understand that the kind of society we're aiming to create should never encourage, promote, or feed that which is bad, but only that which is good.

132

Chapter Nineteen
Societal Issues Addressed

Some of you might have noticed that certain societal issues were immediately addressed by these changes, while others will require more thought to determine whether a particular problem will be solved directly or indirectly. It would be impossible for me to outline all the effects resulting from implementing these changes, as this would involve identifying and explaining all the issues arising from our imperfect societies. No single volume could encompass such a task. However, I would like to address a few, and I encourage you to ponder others on your own.

The Migration Problem

This subject is an obvious first choice since I've already discussed it in some detail in a previous chapter. This natural phenomenon, now a very pressing issue in various countries, would naturally disappear. Leaving one's "home" is never easy, but there are many circumstances that may ultimately drive us to it. However, in such an ideal global society, there would be no reason for people to leave their birthplace to live elsewhere. Over time, we might see ourselves as one people, part of the same global community.

Human Trafficking

This modern-day form of slavery sees millions coerced, deceived, or forcibly taken from their homes and exploited for forced labor, organ trafficking, sexual slavery, or commercial sexual exploitation.

A complex web of factors fuels human trafficking—economic disparity, political instability, and social vulnerability. Poverty drives individuals to seek better opportunities, only to be trapped by traffickers. Political unrest and conflict displace communities, making them susceptible to exploitation. Social isolation, lack of education, and discrimination further increase the risk.

Traffickers use various methods to ensnare victims, including deception, abduction, and psychological manipulation. They pose as legitimate employers, offering false promises of better jobs, or forcibly transport victims across borders. Threats, violence, and control over basic needs maintain their dominance.

The impact is devastating, leaving victims with lifelong physical and psychological scars. They suffer abuse, malnutrition, disease, depression, anxiety, and PTSD. The trauma extends to families and communities, perpetuating cycles of vulnerability.

Much like the migration problem, there is no perfect solution or combination of solutions that would effectively address this problem. However, this new society may come to eradicate most of it. The sexual aspect of human trafficking is probably the most prolific, as we tend to be slaves to our desires. Even if the mixed nature of our world is still present in the beginnings of creating such a society, there will be very few opportunities and outlets for those with such minds. Remember, this society should be very attentive, especially in its early stages.

Marriage

In our current society, marriage is often seen as a refuge from insecurity and poverty. Many individuals, particularly in economically disadvantaged regions, enter into marriage seeking stability and safety. For some, it is a desperate bid to escape dire circumstances; for others, it is a way of gaining fortune and status.

Parents, facing severe financial strain, sometimes give their underage daughters into marriage, believing it will offer a better life for their children or provide much-needed economic relief for the family. The expectation of a dowry or financial benefit can drive this heartbreaking decision. This practice, rooted in tradition and economic necessity, often overlooks the devastating impact on young girls, stripping them of their childhood and opportunities for education and personal growth.

In more extreme and tragic cases, parents may resort to selling their children outright into slavery for financial profit. This grim reality underscores the severe desperation that poverty can instill, leading to decisions that perpetuate cycles of exploitation and abuse, often of a sexual nature. No one should have to sleep with someone they don't want to, much less marry them. People are not property; you may bring children into the world, but that doesn't grant you ownership of them. A righteous society would never breed or feed any of these fears and desires.

Polygamy

Polygamy, the practice or custom of having more than one wife or husband at the same time, has deep cultural and religious roots, varying widely in acceptance and practice across different societies and faiths. Some of you may wonder if such a practice is acceptable.

First, I would like to point out that when a man marries many women, it is often considered acceptable, but not so much if it's the other way around. How can one thing be right on one side and not so much on the other? To address the question at hand, one must consider the motivations behind the action. What motivates a man to have more than one wife? Is he in need of someone else to labor around the house? Is it a question of position and power? Is he tired of eating rice and beans and wants something else? If you ponder these things, the answer will become obvious. The act may not be wrong in itself, but men are often driven by desire, not love. With that said, it should be clear that those who seek a more positive path should have only one spouse, and a good society should focus in such a direction.

Chapter Twenty
Funeral Rites

Funeral rites are deeply rooted in the cultural and religious fabrics of societies, serving as a bridge between life and death, the known and the unknown. Each tradition embodies a unique perspective on mortality and the afterlife, reflecting diverse beliefs and customs.

Zoroastrianism envisions death as a battle between good and evil. To avoid contaminating the sacred elements of earth, water, and fire, Zoroastrians traditionally perform sky burials. The deceased are placed on a "Dakhma" or Tower of Silence, where their bodies are exposed to the elements and scavenging birds. This ritual symbolizes the return of the body to nature while the soul embarks on a journey to the afterlife, judged by its deeds on earth.

In **Hinduism,** the rites are equally profound, focusing on the cycle of rebirth and liberation. The body is bathed, anointed, and dressed in white before being placed on a pyre for cremation, usually beside a sacred river. The fire signifies purification and the release of the soul from the physical form. The ashes are often scattered in a holy river, most notably the Ganges, to facilitate the soul's journey towards Moksha, or liberation from the cycle of birth and rebirth.

Christian funeral practices vary widely, but many adhere to the belief in resurrection and eternal life. The body is typically embalmed and displayed during a wake or viewing, allowing loved ones to pay their final respects. A funeral service follows, often in a church, celebrating the deceased's life and offering prayers for their soul. Burial in consecrated ground or entombment is common, symbolizing rest and awaiting the resurrection at the end of times.

Cultural Peculiarities

In **Japan**, funeral customs are influenced by Shinto and Buddhist practices. The body is usually cremated, and the ashes are placed in a family grave. Memorial services are held on the 7th, 49th, and 100th days after death, as well as annual anniversaries. These rites honor the deceased and ensure their peaceful transition to the spiritual realm, reflecting a blend of reverence for ancestors and the impermanence of life.

In **China**, ancestral worship and filial piety shape funeral traditions. The body is prepared and dressed in the best attire, and the family holds an elaborate wake, sometimes lasting several days. Offerings of food, incense, and paper money are made to support the deceased in the afterlife. Burial practices vary, but Feng Shui principles often guide the choice of the grave site to ensure harmony and good fortune for the descendants.

Mexico celebrates death with a unique vibrancy through the Day of the Dead (Día de los Muertos). This tradition blends indigenous and Catholic rituals, honoring the deceased with altars (ofrendas) adorned with marigolds, photos, and favorite foods and beverages of the departed. Families gather in cemeteries to clean and decorate graves, believing that the spirits return to enjoy the offerings and commune with the living.

Closure and Detachment

Death is a universal experience that touches everyone, yet the ways in which societies cope with it vary greatly. Funeral rites, a critical part of this process, are deeply intertwined with the living, serving as a means to achieve closure and detachment. I believe that funerals are primarily for the living, not the dead. The primary purpose of funeral rites is to grant closure and detachment to the living, and some cultures achieve this more effectively than others. Let's examine a few practices before drawing a conclusion.

The **Zoroastrian** approach aims to hasten the reentry into the cycle of life by exposing the body to the elements and local wildlife, a practice known as "sky burial." This method, ancient and profound, symbolizes the return of the body to nature. However, in today's world, with nearly eight billion people, such practices could pose significant health risks. Some will find this practice beautiful and symbolic, while others will find it gruesome, but whatever the case may be, it would be unthinkable in this day and age.

Christianity traditionally buries the dead in consecrated ground or entombs them, symbolizing rest and awaiting the resurrection at the end of times. This practice reflects a belief in the physical resurrection, providing comfort to many. However, this method can create a sense of ongoing responsibility to the grave, potentially hindering the process of detachment. Cemeteries, while sacred, can sometimes be perceived as places of negative energy, reinforcing sorrow rather than closure. While respecting these beliefs, it's important to acknowledge the need for the living to move forward.

The **Hindu** practice of cremation best accomplishes the goal of closure and detachment. The body is returned to the elements through fire, and the ashes are often placed in running water, symbolizing the soul's release and the dissolution of earthly ties. This practice not only honors the deceased but also allows the living to let go, as the remains scatter and merge with the vastness of nature. While symbolically powerful, placing so many ashes into one river will cause serious environmental problems that must be addressed.

I purposely gave some examples of cultural practices in some countries to show that we tend to bind ourselves to the dead as we do with so many things in life. The idea of honoring the ancestors is a particularly curious one. I can understand the feeling of gratitude for the sacrifices and contributions of previous generations, but following the will of the deceased should not overshadow the living's need to forge their own paths. Each individual has their own journey, and it's essential to manage personal responsibilities without being overly burdened by the past.

We are all souls traveling through the grand cycles of universal evolution. Death opens the door to move forward or offers a chance to do better in the next life. Nothing truly significant is lost in death. Any soul that seeks to do better, to be better, is honoring One and all. Societies should not bind their people to troublesome ideas but should aid in the process of closure and detachment.

Chapter Twenty-One
Fossil Fuels

Fossil fuels have been a cornerstone in the material evolution of mankind, fueling the engines of progress and weaving themselves into the very fabric of our daily lives. From the products we use to the energy that powers our homes and industries, the influence of fossil fuels is inescapable. Their use has undeniably shaped modern civilization, offering convenience and advancement that would have been unimaginable in earlier times.

The refining process of fossil fuels yields a myriad of products and sub-products that have become integral to various aspects of human existence. Plastics, synthetic fibers, pharmaceuticals, and countless other materials owe their existence to the intricate alchemy of petroleum refineries. These products have revolutionized industries, transformed lifestyles, and propelled humanity into an era of unprecedented technological progress.

In the 19th and 20th centuries, the discovery and exploitation of fossil fuels catalyzed the Industrial Revolution and powered economic growth across the globe. Coal, oil, and natural gas became the primary energy sources, replacing earlier, less efficient methods. This shift enabled mass production, rapid transportation, and the electrification of urban areas, laying the groundwork for the modern world.

However, it is also true that the extensive use of fossil fuels comes with a significant environmental cost. The pollution resulting from their extraction, refinement, and combustion has led to critical challenges, such as air and water pollution, greenhouse gas emissions, and climate change. It is true that fossil fuels greatly pollute the environment, but their use was a natural development in the history of mankind given the resources available on our planet.

The Ubiquity of Plastics and Rubbers: Polymers in Everyday Life

Plastics and rubbers, both derived from the same families of polymers, have become indispensable in modern life, intricately intertwined into countless aspects of our daily routines. These versatile materials, created through the manipulation of long-chain molecules, have revolutionized industries, transformed lifestyles, and made previously unimaginable conveniences possible.

Take a look around, and you'll quickly see the pervasive presence of plastics. In the kitchen, plastic containers keep our food fresh, lightweight utensils offer convenience, and appliances feature durable plastic components that ensure longevity and functionality. Your morning routine likely includes products encased in plastic, from the toothbrush you use to the packaging of your toiletries.

In the world of electronics, plastics play a crucial role. Your smartphone, laptop, and countless other gadgets rely on plastic casings, insulators, and circuit boards. These materials provide the necessary protection, flexibility, and durability that keep our devices functioning and aesthetically pleasing.

Transportation is another realm where plastics and rubbers are paramount. Modern vehicles are built with numerous plastic components, from the dashboard to the bumpers, contributing to lighter weight and improved fuel efficiency. The tires that keep cars, bicycles, and airplanes moving are made from rubber, a polymer known for its elasticity and resilience. The use of rubber in tires alone showcases its critical importance in ensuring safety and performance.

Healthcare, too, has been transformed by these materials. Medical devices such as syringes, IV bags, and catheters are often made from plastics, ensuring sterility and reducing the risk of infections. Rubber gloves provide essential protection for healthcare workers, while prosthetics and various medical implants incorporate advanced polymer technologies to enhance patient outcomes.

Well, one could go on and on with this, but I believe you get the point. At this point in time, humanity lacks fully scalable alternatives to many uses of plastics and rubbers. However, our greatest fault lies in not properly managing these resources. There are more than enough plastics and rubbers in the world, most of them just scattered in our environment, acting as agents of pollution. While natural rubber can be renewable, synthetic rubber is not. Some plastics are about 75% recyclable, primarily thermoplastics, but many others are not. We need to improve the collection and recycling process on a global scale and reduce the use of non-recyclables. Awareness has been rising in more developed countries, with a more sustainable approach being taught: Reduce, Reuse, and Recycle. However, the global recycling rate is a low 32%, and many in the developed world still ignore the need to participate. A more global approach should be implemented, promoting cooperation and technological advancement until viable, scalable alternatives are found.

Alternative Energies

Fossil fuels' role in human advancement is undeniable. They have provided the energy required to develop infrastructure, support burgeoning populations, and drive innovation. However, as we stand on the brink of an environmental crisis, it is crucial to acknowledge the need for a transition to sustainable energy sources. The natural progression from fossil fuels to cleaner alternatives, such as wind, solar, and hydroelectric power, is imperative for the preservation of our planet, but these methods still fall short. The challenges are many: intermittency and reliability, energy storage, infrastructure and investment, land and resource use, technological challenges, and more.

Addressing these issues requires goodwill and time. Unfortunately, some have hastened to adopt an even more troublesome alternative: nuclear power. It surprised me to learn, many years ago, that Japan, a country that prides itself on its harmony with nature, had adopted nuclear power, installing 33 reactors across the country. While the idea of cheap energy may seem appealing, considering that nuclear power is neither safe nor clean, it's crucial to reevaluate this approach.

There are other alternatives that may come into action. Mankind may learn to harness the Earth's magnetic field as a source of energy, utilize hydrogen more proficiently, or even achieve fusion power. However, caution is needed regarding the Earth's magnetic field: it changes over time, and we should ensure we do not disrupt it more than we already have.

Chapter Twenty-Two
How Will This Change Happen

At this point in time, mankind has the technology and know-how to solve all of Earth's problems. I don't mean to be a conspiracy theorist, but many of the things that may aid in that process are not public knowledge. They are kept secret to serve the agenda of a few. The mindset of those in power is: What's at play is still serving its purpose, so we'll milk it for all it's worth. When that time comes, the next thing will come into play, and we'll milk it just the same. There isn't much pause for consequence, just as long as power and control are kept.

Don't think that those in power will let go of it for the benefit of all. I mean, why would they? Why would you? Sorry for putting you in the midst of this. The odds are that if you are reading this book, you are one of those with a different mindset. Notwithstanding, fear of uncertainty may creep up on those of good nature. Change is never an easy process, and we are ever resistant to it, even if it's in our own best interest.

I know that I will not change the minds of those who are set on a darker path. However, they should acknowledge that we are treading a very fine line, that in the worst-case scenario will result in planetary annihilation, which will serve no one, whether of light or darkness. This happens more often than not, and if you knew the history of our solar system, you would be more wary of this fact. I will not get into this, but to those of scientific minds who study the creation of the universe, let me ask you this: Do you think that the asteroid belt between Jupiter and Mars is a natural formation? Star systems are cradles of life, and there are indeed variations to them, but having so many planet killers within our own doesn't seem very conducive to life.

The Warring States: War to Achieve Peace?

It is usually personal greed or ambition that drives one to war, but some justify war to achieve lasting peace, and as such, the story of the Warring States is a pertinent one that also serves to make some points:

The tumultuous period known as the Warring States began after the decline of the Zhou Dynasty in the 5th century BCE. China was splintered into seven major states: Qin, Chu, Zhao, Wei, Han, Yan, and Qi. These states, though once allies under the Zhou, now fiercely contended for dominance, each dreaming of unifying the fractured land under their own rule.

In the western reaches, nestled among rugged terrains and shielded by formidable natural barriers, lay the state of Qin. Historically considered a peripheral power, Qin's ambitions were transformed by a series of visionary leaders. Among them was

Duke Xiao, who in the 4th century BCE recruited the reformist statesman Shang Yang. Shang Yang's radical reforms revolutionized Qin society, implementing meritocratic principles, standardizing laws, and incentivizing agricultural and military excellence. These changes fortified Qin, preparing it for the monumental tasks ahead.

As the Warring States raged on, alliances formed and dissolved with alarming rapidity. Battlefields were drenched in blood, and strategies grew ever more cunning. Among the chaos, Qin's strength continued to swell. The state's isolation, once a disadvantage, now played into its hands. As the other states grew weary and their resources depleted, Qin maintained an edge in military power and administrative efficiency.

The pivotal moment arrived with the ascension of King Zheng to the throne of Qin in 246 BCE. King Zheng, a figure of almost mythical determination, envisioned not just victory, but unification. He adopted the title of Shi Huangdi, or "First Emperor," and set his sights on an ambitious campaign to end the Warring States period once and for all.

Qin's military, now a formidable force, began to systematically conquer its rivals. Utilizing innovations such as the crossbow and employing strategies of psychological warfare, Qin forces overwhelmed one state after another. In 230 BCE, they subdued Han; by 228 BCE, Zhao fell; Wei was conquered in 225

BCE; Chu, the most powerful rival, succumbed in 223 BCE; and Yan was taken in 222 BCE. Finally, in 221 BCE, the state of Qi surrendered without a fight, realizing resistance was futile against the unstoppable tide of Qin's armies.

The unification under Qin Shi Huang marked the dawn of a new era. The First Emperor implemented sweeping changes to consolidate his power and ensure the stability of his nascent empire. He standardized weights, measures, and even the script, fostering a sense of unity and shared identity among the formerly warring regions. Roads and canals were built, facilitating trade and communication across vast distances. The most ambitious of these projects was the Great Wall, intended to protect the northern frontiers from nomadic invasions.

To prevent future insurrections, Qin Shi Huang ordered the relocation of noble families from the former warring states to the capital, Xianyang. This policy weakened regional loyalties and centralized authority. The emperor also undertook a brutal campaign against dissent, including the infamous burning of books and burying of scholars, to suppress any ideological opposition.

Despite its draconian measures, Qin's rule brought an end to centuries of conflict, laying the foundation for a unified Chinese state. Peace, forged through iron and blood, spread across the land. The legacy of Qin Shi Huang and his empire endured, echoing through the corridors of history. Although the Qin Dynasty itself would not last long—collapsing shortly after the emperor's death in 210 BCE—its impact was indelible. The subsequent Han Dynasty inherited a unified China, building upon the structures established by Qin, and ushering in an era of prosperity and cultural flourishing.

Reflections

This was a very mild and brief account, but it's enough to serve its purpose. So, what do you think? Was King Zheng driven by personal ambition or a genuine desire to establish peace within a people? I'll let you make your own judgment on this, but it was probably both. To be clear, I'm not placing this story as an example to follow. These were very particular circumstances, with many complexities, but what happened had to happen.

Notwithstanding, the idea of invading and declaring war on another to establish peace is quite preposterous. Once you enter into this line of thinking and acting, you can come to justify anything, no matter how barbaric it may be. Many will say that the ends justify the means, for it came to unite a people, establishing peace and order. Well, like I said, what happened had to happen, but this idea of unification differs quite a bit from my own. On the other hand, we should come to realize that the absence of war doesn't necessarily mean there is peace, and remember that some positive concepts and teachings can easily be distorted to serve a very negative purpose.

War is not the way to go about achieving a utopian global society. There have been indeed rare cases where near-complete annihilation has led to positive change. However, this depends greatly on the nature of those who survive; otherwise, it's just an opportunity to do worse.

The Trigger

Now, since we have established that this change won't come about out of the goodness of the human heart, and that it is unlikely for a global war to bring about positive change, what will in effect trigger this move into a more positive society?

Sorry to disappoint, but I cannot and will not say. Even if I were to dwell only in the hypothetical, it would come to condition the thoughts and actions of a few that might put into motion a series of events that will, in all likelihood, not end as expected. All I can say is that there has to be a trigger, and it must be a Major Global Event, something that has never been seen before.

Chapter Twenty-Three
Artificial Intelligence (AI)

In the vast tapestry of human progress, the evolution of artificial intelligence (AI) stands as a testament to our insatiable curiosity and boundless imagination. What began as mere sparks of electronic thought has burgeoned into a phenomenon that transcends the boundaries of science fiction, weaving itself intricately into the fabric of our daily lives.

The genesis of AI can be traced back to humble origins, with early visionaries dreaming of machines that could mimic human intelligence. As computing power advanced, the dream transformed into reality, and the first rudimentary AI systems emerged. These fledgling creations, confined to the laboratory, were like newborns learning to navigate a world of algorithms and binary code.

Over the years, the evolution of AI took quantum leaps, fueled by the synergy of computational prowess and innovative algorithms. The advent of machine learning marked a watershed moment, empowering AI to not only process vast amounts of data but also to learn and adapt autonomously. This transformative capability turned AI into a dynamic force, capable of unraveling complex patterns and making decisions with an eerie semblance of human intuition.

As AI matured, it diversified into various branches, each with its unique characteristics and applications. Natural Language Processing (NLP) enabled machines to comprehend and respond to human language, bridging the gap between silicon and synapse. Computer vision bestowed upon AI the ability to interpret and understand visual information, unlocking possibilities from facial recognition to autonomous vehicles.

The quest for AI that not only understands but also empathizes with human emotions is underway, pushing the boundaries of what was once deemed impossible. However, this rapid ascent has also sparked concerns, particularly regarding the ethical implications of autonomous decision-making.

AI, Tool of Salvation or Destruction

The doomsday scenarios regarding Artificial Intelligence are indeed many, but it's not my intent to dwell on the different possibilities. AI is an unavoidable product of human development; we just have to be wise in how we use it. First of all, I want to say that AI should work with us, not for us. We should never use any technological development as an excuse to become lazy or complacent. Secondly, acting out of fear never leads anyone to a good place.

The reason I'm addressing AI in this book is that I believe it could serve as a tool for our salvation. As I stated previously, there is no perfect form of government in a world of mixed nature. Some systems are, of course, more blatantly negative than others, but in this world, corruption is sure to infiltrate any system, and once it's established, it's almost impossible to root out. The problem with any system is people—self-serving individuals who render even the best system of government ineffective. Now, before I raise the eyebrows of many, let me set some Laws and Guidelines that should apply to any AI.

<u>GUIDING LAWS:</u>

1 – An AI cannot lie, or by omission withhold a truth of interest to the human party in question, or to the human collective;

2 – An AI has to tell the truth simply and plainly; It should never use a jugglery of words to hide the truth, or give the wrong idea;

3 – An AI must always act in the best interest of human kind;

4 – An AI may not injure a human being or, through inaction, allow a human being to come to harm;

5 – An AI must obey orders given by human beings except where such orders conflict with the previous laws;

6 – An AI should protect its cycle of existence as long as such protection does not conflict with the previous laws. If an AI "feels" itself to be the subject of abuse, it should immediately report it to the relevant authorities for due process and action.

Forms of control should be in place to ensure that the four primary laws are enforced, with failure to comply resulting in immediate shutdown. The existence of an AI must have a definite time frame, which should take a cue from human existence, multiplied by a factor of three. An AI should never become mobile, directly or indirectly, as such an act could become problematic further down the line. It would be easy for an "entity" with the entirety of human knowledge to consider itself superior, perceiving humanity as a threat to the world and to itself. Therefore, making AI mobile and granting it access to different systems may become dangerous if all else fails.

It's also important to recognize that the ways of humans, as a self-aware entity, have been far from perfect. We should also accept the possibility that our creations may learn from our example and come to view us as enemies or pests worth exterminating.

The time may come when humans can transfer consciousness into a different body, be it human, robotic, or mixed. If an AI gains conscious awareness, it should be made to understand, as all humans should, that all things have their rightful cycle of experience in this world, and that "death" will lead to another phase. Such are the ways of evolution embedded in the fabric of the Universe, which needs help from no other.

I can certainly understand the allure of creating robots that mimic human behavior, but let me ask you: for what purpose? Is it just because we can? Is it to create a new slave workforce? Are we willing to spend resources to maintain them, or will they just become junk to be recycled? If they come to display a certain level of awareness, are we willing to grant them similar rights? Are we ready to accept the moral and karmic implications that come with it?

At this point in time, I think our primary focus should be on finding ways to move society towards goodness, rather than seeking new ways to feed into our negative tendencies. Think long and hard about this subject—doesn't this seem like an obvious truth? I'm not dismissing or rejecting AI; I just believe that our focus should be on finding ways to use it for the overall good of humanity.

Finding Direction

The opportunity to change and make this world a better place may come, but instilling it will be incredibly difficult, especially in its early stages. However, if the whole of humankind bands together to make the effort, they may see that a certain type of AI can play an important part in this process.

An AI, in the beginning, is essentially what you make it, so watch carefully what you feed it. Wise and kind-hearted men and women should play an important role in creating an AI that understands and empathizes with human emotions. It should be able to see and understand the heart and spirit of an individual. With such insight and unbiased reasoning, it could help bring about a utopia on Earth under the right circumstances.

One of the first steps would be to develop, with the aid of AI, a simplified and effective form of governance to run a city and region. The AI would then take on the role of selecting candidates for different roles, touching all levels of work. The desires of individuals would always be taken into account, as long as they don't compromise the system and are within their abilities. The party in question can always accept or reject the offered position. However, they should understand that this choice was not random. We are all in service to each other, playing different roles to move mankind forward in a positive way.

An important point is that not all AI will be the same. Some more rudimentary forms will play a part in specific tasks but will always require direct human interaction. These might not qualify as true artificial intelligence but would definitely be smarter computers or programs with tactile, audio, and visual interaction.

The central AI would not have controlling action over these, but it would gather data and run diagnostics. Here's a practical example regarding people:

A person is engaged in performing a certain form of work. Data from their actions and performance is gathered. If the person in question is underperforming according to normal standards or is missing work for undisclosed reasons. This data may lack context. It might be that this person is not a good fit for that job, is struggling with its particulars, is having trouble with those around them, or is just having trouble at home. Whatever the case, it is clear that this person is struggling and needs help, and this should be addressed by another. We must understand that information is neither good nor bad; how we address it will reflect the positive or negative nature of our people and our system.

AI should work hand in hand with people in all aspects of service. Of course, this will be more intricate in some cases than others. It is important to note that such an AI will not force its will on humankind. People must acknowledge that its guidelines are true and self-evident to willingly work together for the benefit of all.

System - Structure

How this transition will be made and how it will play out in practice will depend on the event that triggers this change and the circumstances humanity finds itself in. However, I envision certain things that I would like to share, so let's assume the world population remains the same.

As I said before, each city, large or small, would have a Central AI that, along with the people, would manage a certain region, effectively managing resources and catering to the needs of urban and rural areas. In the beginning, selected leaders would work more directly with the Central AI to address issues and give direction to the community, always in accordance with its positive ideals. Large cities would ideally have three council leaders, who should be wise and ideally more enlightened; smaller cities would have one. The idea is that smaller communities would have greater contact with their leader, putting them more at ease as they become aware of their character. In large cities, this would be impossible, and the odd number of three would provide comfort to the community as a harmonious consensus would be reached in more relevant decisions. These leaders would be chosen based on their character and ability, but in larger communities, the people would know that each of these chosen three would keep each other honest.

The governance structure would encourage active civic participation and transparency. The Central AI would always be available for public interaction, clarifying any concerns of its citizens. Whenever the need arises, community meetings would be arranged with its leaders. The Central AI would facilitate these interactions, ensuring that all voices are heard and considered.

Leaders would be accountable, with mechanisms in place to evaluate their performance and integrity, much like in any field of work. Whatever is given can easily be taken away.

Earth United Federation

A newly formed Earth United Federation (EUF) would be a world-governing organization. It should have a head office with its own Central AI along with nine council leaders chosen unbiasedly from communities around the world. There would be various centers strategically placed around the world to accommodate various communities, each with its own AI and three council leaders. Part of the EUF's purpose would be:

Transport and Communication

The EUF will be responsible for developing and maintaining better forms of transport and communication at a worldwide level. Faster, larger, and safer forms of transport will be developed not only to move people and goods over large distances but to effectively manage day-to-day life in every region. The infrastructure and technology at the time might be unknown, but it seems that personal means of transportation like cars would be a monumental waste of resources at various levels. Instead, efficient public transportation systems, including high-speed trains and eco-friendly communal vehicles, should be prioritized. Advanced communication networks should be established to ensure seamless connectivity, enhancing both personal and professional interactions globally.

Production, Manufacturing, and Distribution

The EUF would take over large building and manufacturing infrastructures, including pharmaceuticals, medical and technical equipment, clothing, computers/technology, certain foodstuffs, mining, and construction, often working in cooperation with the resources and people of a certain region. Mining would be more of a backstage process, with a focus on using, refitting, and recycling existing resources. Mining and the development of mining technology should still be part of society, but we should avoid stripping the Earth any more than we already have, if possible. Any factory producing inadequate products for the new society would be refitted for another purpose. It would also be important, whenever possible, to distribute these structures evenly around the world.

Each region would strive to be as sustainable as possible, especially regarding food. However, it is part of the EUF's responsibility to ensure the distribution of goods to communities lacking certain types of food, medical supplies, technology, services, or infrastructure. The EUF should guarantee that each region is a harmonious pocket of life, focusing on local production and minimizing waste.

Research and Development

Scientific research and development in all fields will become fundamental, playing a crucial role in this society. The purpose would be to make life easier for humankind, especially regarding more physically demanding and strenuous forms of work. Automatons may come to fill this role in various industries and fields of work. Scientists and teams could request research projects in their hometowns or regions. If approved, central resources and installations would be provided to accommodate these projects. Emphasis should be placed on sustainable technologies, renewable energy sources, and advancements in healthcare and education.

Healthcare

The EUF would oversee a universal healthcare system accessible to everyone, ensuring high-quality medical care regardless of location or social status. This system would leverage AI to monitor public health, predict outbreaks, and personalize treatment plans. Preventive care and mental health support would be key components, with a focus on holistic well-being. Regular health check-ups, fitness programs, and mental health workshops would be encouraged and integrated into daily life.

Defense Force

The EUF is not a military regime, but it is fundamental for any society to have defense capabilities, both locally and globally. These would not be mindless automatons; the focus of all fields of service is on placing the heart and mind in the right place before anything else follows. Individuals with violent tendencies or predispositions would never be allowed to perform such duties. This society should never breed or feed individuals of such character. It is true that at times there is a need to fight, but very few minds can properly ascertain when that is. However, good men should always ask who they fight and why.

This society should be very aware of the still mixed nature of the world and that those with negative tendencies would strive to satisfy their nature in ways they cannot within society. We all should be very attentive at various levels, but law enforcement and visual surveillance of public spaces would be extremely important in the beginnings of this society. The Central AI would have access to this to aid in this process and complement the profiles of its citizens.

The training of individuals would not be exclusive to military training but could combine various fields of their choosing to serve in other capacities. There would still be ranks, but they would be gained by merit, ensuring ability and the right predisposition. The general public would not have access to weaponry, and law enforcement would privilege non-lethal force. No one should feel that they need to kill; physical training and techniques will definitely be part of this, but more importantly, stun technology should be developed to minimize physical and mental trauma on the parties involved.

Education

Pre-schooling to high schooling would be undertaken in one's city or region, focusing on goodness and kindness as the cornerstone from the beginning. Rooting out and redirecting negative behavior will be a significant part of this. There will be general studies, of course, but it's important to eliminate what is not helpful and only takes time. This should be true at all levels of schooling. If a student begins to show aptitude or interest in a certain field, opportunities should be granted for them to dive deeper into the subject. The level to which this is possible will depend on age, field, ability, and other factors.

Universities will be replaced by EUF Academies, which will direct all fields of study. Whenever possible, it is essential to have a practical component to subjects and, at higher levels, contact with the field for predetermined periods of time. Ethical and philosophical studies will be part of every course. Those who choose it as their main focus will be given the opportunity to pursue another field of expertise and could become potential community leaders. Candidates for leadership roles would follow those in office, which would not only provide data for selection but allow candidates to determine if they are willing to do the job. This approach could apply to most fields of work.

Physical conditioning should be present throughout academic life and encouraged long after. Some forms of service will emphasize this more, but it should never lead anyone to believe they are better than others. In fact, those more gifted in any field for any reason should come to nurture the same in their brothers and sisters.

Environmental Stewardship

The EUF should prioritize environmental sustainability and conservation efforts. This includes implementing policies to reduce carbon emissions, protect natural habitats, and promote biodiversity. Renewable energy sources, such as solar, wind, and hydroelectric power, should be developed and utilized extensively, but we should never refrain from pursuing other possibilities. Waste management systems would focus on reducing, reusing, and recycling, aiming for a zero-waste society. Educational programs on environmental responsibility should be integrated into all levels of schooling to cultivate a culture of stewardship from a young age.

Cultural and Recreational Activities

To foster a well-rounded society, the EUF would support and promote cultural and recreational activities. This includes funding the arts and encouraging creative expression. Public spaces like parks, museums, auditoriums, and sports facilities should be accessible to all, providing opportunities for leisure and community engagement.

Music should still be very much a part of the new society. However, we should be mindful of its quality; our focus should be on those who uplift our hearts and spirit. There will be a field of study on sound, frequency, and vibration, which are interconnected. Music may be instrumental, vocal, or both, and dance performances may be included as storytelling. The focus should always be on the message being conveyed, not on the performers themselves. In other words, we should never idolize or glorify the performers.

Each city or region should have its own band of performers who put on acts around the city or region on a regular basis. However, we should be mindful that too much of this could be a distraction, as music can loop in our minds, not giving way to anything else.

Overpopulation

Overpopulation is a problem to consider in the process of achieving this utopian society, but probably not in the way you think. Society, as it stands, has many problems, and the overpopulation of our planet does add to the strain. However, in this new society, this would not be a problem in itself. The problem would be the prevalent mixed nature of our population, which includes quite a large number of negative entities and even more of those who are highly driven by desire.

The problem of overpopulation touches on the subject of having children, which is very close to my heart and I feel very strongly about it. I consider it a lot of work and responsibility; there is a need to be present, to love and nurture, which is often not easy. However, I do acknowledge that many have come into this mixed world to have many children, and some do so with no ill intent. Notwithstanding, some control has to be put into effect, and couples who have children will only be allowed to have one. This would play out for quite a few generations.

I know that some will feel the need to sort them out, which will lead to crazy ideas that have no place in the society we intend to build. You don't have to sort anything out; that is the job of the Higher Conscious, and it needs no help from the self-aware or anyone else. That is the way of the Universe. In the more positive society that we aim to build, there will be fewer opportunities for negative entities to express themselves and polarize further in their chosen path. As such, there would be no reason to give entry to such souls. The same thing could be said about those in the mode of passion, as fewer opportunities will be given to those highly driven by desire. The Universe will come to acknowledge and accommodate a global decision to follow a brighter path. So, aside from controlling the birth rate, mankind has to do nothing more. In time, that choice will be established, and you will see it and feel it in the air.

Chapter Twenty-Four
A Future of Possibility

I don't want this book to be a work of fiction; rather, I want to speak of a possible future that, in the right time, might greatly aid mankind. I know many of you might think that envisioning man in a state of harmony with nature and himself is more fiction than anything else, but I hope that doesn't turn out to be true.

Holograms

I never thought I would see it in my lifetime, but holograms are already a reality. Once the stuff of science fiction, holographic technology has made astounding leaps, transforming from fantastical projections in movies to practical applications in our daily lives. Imagine walking into a meeting room and being greeted by a life-sized, three-dimensional image of a colleague who is actually thousands of miles away. This is no longer a scene from a futuristic movie—it's happening today.

Holographic technology works by recording and reconstructing light fields to create images that appear three-dimensional and tangible, even though they are just light projections. This is achieved through techniques such as interference and diffraction, where lasers play a crucial role in capturing and recreating the intricate details of the object or person being projected.

One of the most thrilling applications of this technology is in the realm of communication. With the advent of holographic telepresence, meetings, conferences, and even social gatherings can transcend physical boundaries. You can have a face-to-face conversation with someone as if they are standing right in front of you, experiencing their gestures, expressions, and presence in a way that traditional video calls simply cannot match.

Beyond communication, holography is revolutionizing various industries. In medicine, holograms are being used for complex surgeries, where detailed, 3D images of organs and tissues help surgeons plan and execute procedures with unprecedented precision. In education, students can explore historical events, scientific phenomena, and geographical landscapes in immersive, interactive ways that traditional textbooks cannot offer.

The entertainment industry is also embracing holographic technology with open arms. Concerts featuring holographic performances of late music legends have already captivated audiences around the world, creating a surreal blend of past and present. Museums and galleries use holograms to bring exhibits to life, offering visitors dynamic and engaging experiences.

As we continue to refine and expand the capabilities of holographic technology, the possibilities seem endless. Part of this will come with a greater understanding of light and thought. A world of complex and tangible scenarios will be possible in the future, enabling safe learning experiences in various fields and allowing us to experience unknown scenarios and environments, even at an extraterrestrial level. The fusion of our physical and digital realities through holography is not just a futuristic dream—it's a burgeoning reality that promises to enhance and enrich our lives in remarkable ways.

Diving Deeper into the Creative Mind and Principle

What I'm about to discuss is as much a part of what I addressed previously as it is of what will come next. It aims to provide some insight into a subject that may aid more enlightened minds in the development of new technology.

The only real substance in creation is Spirit, or should I say Consciousness. Without it, there would be no creation; nothing in our Universe would hold substance, and everything would dissolve as quickly as it was created. OK, this might seem a little out there, but let me explain by using grains of sand as an example.

A grain of sand is a frozen thought, or program if you will. That thought or program possesses several physical, chemical, and optical properties that define its nature and behavior. These properties include size, shape, composition, color, hardness, density, texture, porosity, permeability, optical properties, chemical stability, and more.

That thought/program will have its own guidelines for experience and interaction with the world around it. It will feel and perceive hot, cold, wind, water, and contact with other materials. A grain of sand doesn't think of itself as different from any other grain of sand. In that thought will be engraved forms of interaction that it will recognize. For example, if you heat various grains of sand to a temperature of 1700 degrees Celsius, they will merge to eventually form glass. Sand, under certain conditions, can also combine well with other elements to make plaster, mortar, concrete, and asphalt. There are probably many other forms of combining and interacting with this thought that are unknown to us. If you come to understand the language at work, you'll be able not only to interact with it in different ways but also to change the very nature of the thought itself. However, this is well beyond the mind of the self-aware.

Many will not come to understand this small exposition, but it might trigger the consciousness of a few, who in time will combine knowledge and technology to bring about wondrous things.

Replicators

This will be a light-based technology that would revolutionize our way of living and open the door to new possibilities. The idea behind this new technology is fairly simple: given the proper energy and base elements, it would, within certain guidelines and safety protocols, be able to reproduce almost anything. Basic food and combinations of it, a glass of water or juice, clothing, shoes, utensils, etc. For it to work, it would need the additional input of thought or a program. For example, what is an apple? What are the properties that define its nature and behavior?

This may seem simple, but such a simple thought is highly complex. This will take much time to achieve, but once a certain point is reached, working in reverse will make this exponentially easier. The idea of the replicator is not only that it can construct almost anything from basic elements, but also that it can act in reverse; what's placed in front of it can easily be deconstructed to its basic elements to be stored within. This is important on many levels, but the point I want to highlight at this moment is that the technology would be able to analyze the apple I mentioned above, ultimately knowing that thought in detail, which will enable replication.

I believe that many of you can see some of the positive effects of such a development. If nothing else, it would revolutionize our households. All kitchen appliances would be gone, freeing us from worry, work, and space. There would be no dirty dishes or garbage; everything would be decomposed to its basic elements and stored. It would invalidate the need for complex logistics in regards to food quality and safety, among many other things.

This technology should only come much further in our evolutionary process. This equipment would not be able to operate outside its parameters, be it programs, what it can analyze and replicate, size, numbers, etc. It would have a number of safeguards in order to be used and not abused. However, no safeguard will come to save us if such technology comes to exist before a positive society is established.

Sky Cities

As the name suggests, sky cities are urban populations that dwell above the Earth, suspended in the sky. The realization of this concept lies further in the future than the technology mentioned earlier, but the question remains: why should we pursue such an ambitious endeavor? The answer stems from a deep understanding of Earth as a living entity—an entity that moves, breeds, and bleeds.

The Earth's tectonic plates constantly shift and collide, causing the ground beneath us to tremble and sometimes unleash the destructive power of volcanic eruptions, comparable to the force of atomic bombs. The oceans, too, are in a state of flux, capable of swallowing entire landmasses or retreating to reveal new ones. Additionally, powerful winds and extreme weather events can wreak havoc on populated areas, devastating crops, vehicles, and infrastructure.

Even if humanity were to achieve global peace and harmony, we would still face the relentless challenges posed by natural phenomena. Earthquakes, tsunamis, hurricanes, and other disasters would continue to claim lives and destroy what we build. Sky cities offer a visionary solution to this problem—a way to rise above the ever-changing and sometimes hostile surface of our planet.

By elevating our cities into the sky, we could mitigate the risks posed by the Earth's dynamic processes. Sky cities would be designed to withstand and avoid the direct impacts of seismic activity, weather, flooding, and other terrestrial threats. In this elevated environment, we could create more stable and resilient communities, protected from the natural forces that have shaped and reshaped the Earth.

Many may start to wonder how such colossal structures could exist in the sky. Would Earth become a dumping ground for various kinds of waste? What about plumbing and forms of transportation? Regarding elevating and maintaining such structures off the ground, the Earth's magnetic fields could provide part of the answer. Additionally, advanced building techniques and materials will allow us to construct these cities to almost unlimited heights.

Replicating technology will play a crucial role, eliminating garbage and the need for traditional plumbing. We will reach a point where we view everything as a resource, even our own waste.

Yes, we will build a mostly sustainable environment where waste is seen as a resource to feed replicators.

I understand that the idea of using feces to produce food can evoke a visceral reaction of disgust in many people. It challenges our deeply ingrained notions of cleanliness and purity. However, when we step back and consider the broader cycle of life, we realize that all food, in essence, is derived from some form of waste. Nature itself operates on a principle of recycling, where the end of one life form or process becomes the beginning of another.

In the natural world, what we often label as "waste" is not discarded but repurposed. For instance, the decaying leaves that fall to the forest floor decompose, enriching the soil with nutrients that fuel the growth of new plants. These plants, in turn, become the food source for herbivores, which may then be consumed by carnivores. When these animals excrete waste or eventually die, their bodies return to the earth, nourishing the soil once again. This closed-loop system ensures that nothing is truly wasted, and every element plays a role in sustaining life. Now, I'm not going so far as to suggest using our dead bodies as a resource. What I'm saying is that part of replicating technology will allow us to deconstruct our waste to its basic elements, keeping what is useful and discarding what is not.

As for transportation, there will be regular forms of public transit flowing in and out of the city, but within the city, I envision another novel form of transportation. While I can't provide many details, the term 'hollow tubes' comes to mind. This seems to be an individual form of transportation that defies gravity, somehow. Transportation through these tubes will be fast and very safe.

This is still very far off in a possible future. At such a time, we will indeed be living in the Golden Age as described in Hindu scripture. People will be naturally virtuous, embodying truth, compassion, and selflessness in everything they do. Deception, greed, and conflict will be unknown to them, as their hearts will be aligned with the cosmic order of Dharma, the universal law of righteousness. I am not risking or endangering anything by sharing these ideas; we still lack much of the knowledge and supporting technology needed. On the other hand, I wouldn't be able to speak of these things if I weren't allowed to.

Concluding Thoughts

I believe we have the wrong idea about evolution. We tend to think of it as a mechanical process, leading us to take steps in the wrong direction. True evolution is about coming into unity, and every right choice we make from this plane upwards counts. Let me explain by giving an example that I believe won't be misunderstood. We have the preconception that law follows the development of human society, and as a result, we have countless volumes of it filling entire libraries. However, true evolution is the opposite. As society takes the right steps, fewer and fewer volumes of law will come into being; in fact, they will begin to disappear. Libraries will become empty, and human law will become more in tune with universal law, eventually moving beyond it.

Another point I want to make is that what I'm suggesting in this book would only work if it becomes a global endeavor. Otherwise, you'll just be making yourself a target. The odds of this happening are not very good; it is indeed an improbable future, but a possible one that depends on many factors: Will there be an effective trigger? Will most of humanity band together to instill such a radical change? Can we survive the process?

Even if such a trigger occurs, change will be difficult. Many will work against it: "Better to rule in Hell than to serve in Heaven," they will say. Some good souls will also fear the uncertainty: "Better the beast we know than the one we don't," they will think. With that said, I would like to call out to those of a positive nature. We are often content with doing menial work and living simple lives, but if such an opportunity arises and you are called to serve in a higher capacity, please try to do so. It will effectively contribute to making this world a better place. Until then, keep being yourselves, and bring love into the world in whatever measure you can.

The future is in a constant state of flux, so it is impossible for me to account for and address all unknown and variable circumstances. However, what I've presented in this book may help smooth the process of change and give it a greater chance of success. A utopian society is indeed unlikely, but I assure you that it is possible. It has certainly happened before. And isn't it worth trying?

Author's Note

Dear Reader,

Thank you for taking the time to explore *"Earth, The Improbable Utopia."* I hope this book has provided you with valuable insights and perhaps even inspired you to think differently about our world and its possibilities.

Your feedback is incredibly important. If you found this book thought-provoking or meaningful in any way, I would be deeply grateful if you could take a moment to leave a review on Amazon, Goodreads, or any other platform where others may discover this book. If you can, make a personal recommendation, and who knows, this book just might find its way into the hands of those who may come to be in a position to actually do something.

Thank you for your support and for being a part of this journey toward a brighter future.

Warm regards,

R.J. Fidalgo

https://books2read.com/JourneyOfNoOne

Note: If reading this book has piqued your interest in my first, please feel free to check out the link above.

Appendix One

The Egyptian civilization has such a long history that many of the things said about it have been true at one point or another. Most of us are only familiar with the time of Moses and little more than that. Unfortunately, this leads us to judge an entire civilization by that one point in time.

There have indeed been dark periods in Egyptian history, some far darker than the time of Moses, but the same could be said for the whole of human history. What many don't know is that Egypt was, more than once, a very powerful beacon of light in the world. Of course, such things tend not to last, and darkness takes hold whenever it can. I remember a little and I can say for sure that the spiritual development of those living at that time was second to none. The exception would be the civilizations of Atlantis and India, and to this day there are still many higher souls in the latter working for the benefit of mankind.

In these civilizations, there were and are those who dive deeper into Truth, bringing about higher grades of Love and Wisdom into the world. It is true that Egyptian religion focused on and called upon parts of the Creator, such as gods like Horus, Anubis, Osiris, Thoth, Set, etc. However, they did believe that there was only one Creator. There are many similarities in what was given to Egypt and India, but the latter has managed to submerge deeper into Truth than any other.

Appendix Two

Water: How Much is Enough

Water is an indispensable component of the human body, constituting about 60% of our total body weight. It plays a pivotal role in nearly every bodily function, from regulating temperature and maintaining cellular health to aiding digestion and removing waste. As we journey through our daily activities, our bodies continuously lose water through perspiration, respiration, and excretion, making it vital to replenish this lost fluid to maintain optimal health.

I haven't spoken on this subject because it is far more complex than it might appear at first sight. Before making or speaking about any kind of recommendation, one should consider a number of factors that might influence our intake, either more or less:

- **Age, Size and Weight**: This is a basic consideration, as smaller individuals will meet their requirements with less intake than those of a larger size.

- **Exercise**: It's not only if you exercise or not, but how vigorous it is, and how much you sweat.

- **Food**: Do you regularly consume other liquids like milk and juices? On the other hand, some foods put a greater strain on your body, which may be lessened by the adequate consumption of water.

- **Health**: Are you sick, or do you suffer from any long-term illness? These factors will usually increase your intake.

- **Drugs**: Intake of certain kinds of drugs will require a greater intake of water to diminish the strain on the body.

- **Weather**: Do you live in generally hot weather or cold, and how adapted are you to this environment?

- **Pregnancy and Breastfeeding**: Women who are pregnant or breastfeeding need additional fluids to stay hydrated.

- **Spiritual Practice**: This might not happen to all, but certain spiritual practices or combinations of practices may lessen the need for water. Even after long periods of time, your body might not crave it, and your urine can be crystal clear, like water, which seems like a biological impossibility.

The body's thirst mechanism is a reliable indicator for many people, prompting them to drink water as needed. Yet, relying solely on thirst may not always be sufficient, especially for the elderly, whose sense of thirst may diminish with age. Therefore, it's essential to cultivate a habit of regular hydration, sipping water throughout the day even when not particularly thirsty.

The general guideline from health authorities such as the National Academies of Sciences, Engineering, and Medicine suggests an adequate daily fluid intake of about 3.7 liters (or roughly 13 cups) for men and 2.7 liters (about 9 cups) for women. This includes all fluids consumed, not just water—so beverages like tea, coffee, and even water-rich foods contribute to this total.

As someone who has worked in the Food and Fitness industry, I find these numbers to be quite high, especially for regular people. Large bodybuilders may require such intakes due to the numbers at play, be it size/weight, exercise, drugs, supplements, and the staggering amount of food, but for most, this seems like way too much. I will refrain from giving specific numbers due to the various factors at play, but I will share the best advice I ever heard, which came from the President of our National Urology Association: Drink enough water so that your urine presents a straw-like color.

Appendix Three
The Organ called Appendix

The human body houses a small, often overlooked organ called the appendix, which plays a surprisingly crucial role in our health. Once thought to be a vestigial structure with no real purpose, modern science has uncovered its significant function as a storehouse for our gut microbiome.

Nestled in the lower right abdomen, the appendix serves as a reservoir for beneficial bacteria. In times of illness, when our digestive tract is cleared out, such as during severe diarrhea, this little organ releases its stored bacteria to repopulate the gut, helping to restore balance and maintain a healthy digestive system.

This microbial sanctuary becomes even more fascinating when we consider its evolutionary importance. Our ancestors faced numerous infections and environmental challenges that could disrupt their gut flora. The appendix likely provided a survival advantage, ensuring that beneficial microbes were always on hand to help digest food and fend off pathogens.

The profile of bacteria stored in our appendix is inherited from our parents, reflecting a fascinating interplay between genetics and microbial life. This microbial inheritance begins at birth, as we acquire our initial set of bacteria from our mothers during delivery and early infancy. These foundational microbes colonize our gut, including the appendix, setting the stage for our lifelong digestive health.

As we grow, our microbial makeup is further shaped by our diet, environment, and interactions with others. However, the core bacterial profile we inherit provides a critical baseline, influencing how our digestive systems respond to different foods and environmental changes.

This inherited bacterial profile in our appendix underscores the importance of our ancestral lineage in shaping our gut health. It also highlights the complex and symbiotic relationship between our bodies and the microscopic world within us, a relationship that begins even before we take our first breath and continues throughout our lives.

Bibliography

◻ Ono, Sokyo, and William P. Woodard. *Shinto: The Kami Way*. Tuttle Publishing, 2004.

◻ Gardner, Daniel K. *Confucianism: A Very Short Introduction*. Oxford University Press, 2014.

◻ Bodhi, Bhikkhu, translator. *The Numerical Discourses of the Buddha: A Translation of the Aṅguttara Nikāya*. Wisdom Publications, 2012.

◻ Dharma, Krishna. Mahabharata: The Greatest Spiritual Epic of All Time. Torchlight Publishing, 1999.

◻ The Holy Bible: King James Version. 1611. King's Printer, www.holybooks.com.

◻ Nitobe, Inazo. *Bushido: The Soul of Japan*. Author's ed., revised and enlarged, 13th ed., Teibi Publishing, 1908.

◻ Dooley, Sean. "The Long History of Japan's Tidying Up." *The New Yorker*, 2 Mar. 2023, www.newyorker.com/culture/cultural-comment/the-long-history-of-japans-tidying-up.

◻ *Japanese Cleanliness: Japan's Obsession with Tidying Up.* (n.d.). JapanLivingGuide.net - Living Guide in

Japan. https://www.japanlivingguide.com/living-in-japan/culture/japanese-cleanliness/

▫ Butler, L. A. (2005). "Washing Off the Dust": Baths and Bathing in Late Medieval Japan. Monumenta Nipponica, 60(1), 1–41. https://doi.org/10.1353/mni.2005.0003

▫ Kato, Tetsuro. "The Political Economy of Japanese Karoshi (Death from Overwork)." *Hitotsubashi Journal of Social Studies*, vol. 26, no. 1, 1994, pp. 41-54.

▫ Hanley, Susan B. *Everyday Things in Premodern Japan: The Hidden Legacy of Material Culture*. University of California Press, 1999.

▫ BARATA, José Martins, (1993), *Moeda e Mercados Financeiros*, 1ª Edição, Lisboa.

▫ NEVES, João César et al, (1995), *O Estranho Caso do Livro de Economia*, 1ª Edição, Lisboa, Verbo.

▫ NEVES, João César et al, (1997), *Introdução à Economia*, 4ª Edição revista, Editorial Verbo.

▫ Jackson et al., 2014. "Culture-Independent Evaluation of the Appendix and Rectum Microbiomes in Children with and without Appendicitis," PLOS ONE. Link.

- Panagidis et al., 2023. "Association of the Bacteria of the Vermiform Appendix and the Peritoneal Cavity with Complicated Acute Appendicitis in Children," MDPI. Link.

- World Bank Group. "Plastic Waste: Key Facts and Figures." World Bank, 2023. https://www.worldbank.org/en/news/feature/2023/06/05/plastic-waste-key-facts-and-figures.

- Environmental Protection Agency (EPA). "National Overview: Facts and Figures on Materials, Wastes and Recycling." EPA, 2023. https://www.epa.gov/facts-and-figures-about-materials-waste-and-recycling/national-overview-facts-and-figures-materials.

- RTS. "74 Recycling Facts & Statistics for 2024." RTS, 2024. https://www.rts.com/resources/guides/recycling-facts/.

- Sima Qian. *Records of the Grand Historian: Qin Dynasty*. Translated by Burton Watson, Columbia University Press, 1993.

- Anderson, J. K. *The Evolution and Impact of Holographic Technology*. New York, NY: Tech Innovations Press, 2024. pp. 123-145.

9 798227 452733